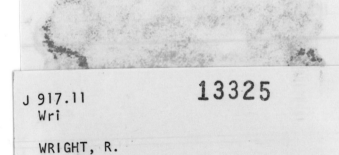

CARIBOO MILEPOSTS

Points of Interest Along a Famous Road.

Richard & Rochelle Wright

MITCHELL PRESS

Printed in Canada

*Dedicated to all who gave us
encouragement and help to do
the things we knew and loved.*

Foreword

Cariboo Mileposts is not meant to be a definitive, historical work on the Cariboo region, but rather an attempt to show a few of the places of interest that are left, along with something of their history, the geology and the flora and fauna of the country. We hope to arouse interest and to encourage further reading in the various subjects, for only by many people being aware of the very special attributes of this historical area can they be protected. For this reason we have suggested a number of books which deal with the area in more detail.

Our sources of information have been many and varied and have been gathered over a period of three years. Consequently, there could well be a few minor errors as to first names and similar small details. In the case of legends or stories handed down through time we have chosen those that seem the most plausible or accurate. Some have been included because of interest. We know they are not true as will the reader. Often there are many variations of stories concerning one particular incident. If any reader can give additional information we would be most pleased to hear from you. Only in this way can we hope to correct or add to what has been written. Hopefully in a future edition these facts could be included.

Mileages are as accurate as we can make them. Every year the highway is being improved and straightened and thereby usually shortened. However, the traveller can take this into account and should still be able to locate the points mentioned.

Richard and Rochelle Wright
Port Moody, B.C.
October 1971

Symbols

  Mileages and Directions

  Historical Reference

  Stop-of-Interest Sign

  Plants, Wildlife and Geology

  Miscellaneous Item of Interest

Acknowledgements

The writing of a book such as this actually involves many more people than those whose names appear on the cover. Were it not, first of all, for the early settlers and pioneers this work would naturally never have appeared. Fortunately there have been, through time, people who took the time to write things down, the happenings and stories of their days and the things they remember from childhood. To these people we are thankful. Then there are those who have answered our letters and queries and given of their knowledge. Molly Forbes of Lac La Hache has told of the many Road Houses and families in that area; Harold Mitchell, Regional Wildlife Biologist at Williams Lake, was our source for some of the wildlife information; Dennis Demarchi, Wildlife Biologist in Victoria, gave us information on the vegetation; Leo Van Tine, John Lesowski and Pat Mulligan, formerly of Williams Lake, told us about the country and some of their stories; Keith Smith, wildlife artist, who has painted much of the Cariboo, travelled with us and gave us ideas, encouragement and information. And Edd Wright, Richard's brother, has done a lot of typing and travelling for us and with us. Thanks, too, go to the many people to whom we have spoken in museums, lodges, and on the roadsides. Finally, we are indebted to Chess Lyons, whose early books on B.C. primed our interest in this province of B.C. and the outdoors.

All photographs are by the authors unless otherwise credited.

Introduction

The modern Cariboo Highway from Cache Creek to Barkerville
is an adventure road through history. It is a 260-mile journey
where the visitor can spend a long weekend following
the original road to the mines, a two-week vacation exploring
a few of its many attractions, or an entire summer
in a region that is an exciting blend of history and nature.

The logical place to start a journey through this historic
country is Mile Zero of the Cariboo Highway. Locating
Mile Zero, however, can be a problem since there have been
three "Cariboo Roads". The earliest started at Lillooet,
where the Harrison Trail from the coast ended, and
was built in 1861. The roadhouses from there to Clinton and from
Clinton north all took their names from that mileage.
In 1863 the Yale-Cariboo Waggon (sic) Road was built and
Yale became portal to the Cariboo. Then with completion
of the Canadian Pacific Railway in 1886, Ashcroft
became gateway to the Cariboo and the gold fields. New

roadhouses and ranches from Ashcroft to Clinton used Ashcroft as Mile Zero. And if that isn't confusing enough, today Cache Creek is generally accepted as Mile Zero, even though roadhouses from Clinton use the original 1859 mileage from Lillooet.

Anyone coming from the Lower Mainland of Vancouver and wishing to follow the original route from Lillooet can leave the Trans-Canada Highway at Lytton in the Fraser Canyon. The road from Lillooet to Clinton is listed as a side trip at Mile 25.

In order to maintain some type of continuity and travel in a generally northerly direction, the book and our journey begin at Ashcroft Manor, taking the side road to Ashcroft back to the Cariboo Highway. We then pick up Mile Zero at Cache Creek, the start of the modern Cariboo Highway.

At mile 0 — Cache Creek. Bonaparte House on Cache Creek. The present highway passes behind the building. It was located near where the present road crosses the creek and where the old road joins the pavement. Note the different spelling of Semlin on the sign. Vancouver City Archives photo.

Mileposts

The original mileposts of the Cariboo Road were squared timbers, 12 to 14 inches square with 'housed' tops to shed the rain. Just when these were set up is not on record but the posts gave mileages from Lillooet and Yale. In 1899, however, the provincial government decided to establish new posts. Who got the contract is unsure, but the work was done by Anson Milo Bushnell, a horse-trading homesteader living below Clinton on Dan Smith's Lake (later noted for its Epsom salts). His job was to measure the road from Ashcroft to Barkerville, a distance of 280 miles, now shortened to 266.

To measure the mileage he fashioned a barrow of sorts, made from a bicycle wheel, a cyclometer and a set of handles from a barroom chair. On a small platform in front he carried his few requirements, consisting of a set of stencils, an axe, a change of clothes and a yellow slicker. He then started up the center of the road, erecting a short 12 inch stake at every mile.

Since most of the Mile Houses were named with Lillooet as Mile Zero and had been in business for some 30 years, owners were unwilling to change the mileage and therefore the name of their stopping place. Consequently today the roadhouses and communities such as 100 Mile House reflect the distance from Lillooet.

Eventually these rather hasty 'posts' had to be replaced, first by 'Old Bush' himself and then by the Department of Public Works who erected proper white and black signs.

Mile 0

CACHE CREEK   Situated at the junction of the Cariboo Highway 97 and the Trans-Canada 1 to Kamloops and points east.

There are many stories as to how the name Cache Creek originated but in the Akriggs' book, '1001 B.C. Place Names', they give the most plausible. The Akriggs discount the stories of miners caching gold here and similarly the tale of a lone robber being shot and hiding his loot. They point out that in the account of Commander R. C. Mayne, R.N., which he wrote on his journey from Fort Kamloops to Pavilion in 1859, the name is used. He wrote, "We left the Thompson and camped for the night by the side of Rivière de la Cache, a small stream flowing into the Bonaparte." Gold had not yet been discovered, so all that can be said is that prior to 1859 someone — probably the early fur traders — obviously cached something in the area.

A typical Cariboo scene of a Russell fence, cattle and pine trees.

A cache can be two things. Today it means a place where food and provisions are kept out of animals' reach, usually on a high platform. The fur-traders' cache was a hole in the ground, shaped like a bottle and lined with dry grass and branches. When the top or turf was replaced there was no evidence of the hiding place.

The first hotel in Cache Creek stood where the Bert Collins home now stands, just north of the highway crossing Cache Creek and was built by James Orr. It was originally erected near Rattlesnake Mountain, but was purchased by Semlin and Parke, moved to the new location and renamed Bonaparte House. In 1868 Parke sold his share to W. H. Sanford of Boston Flats and the house was run under the name Semlin and Sanford for a few more years.

Cache Creek was also the site of the first boarding school in the Interior of B.C. It was opened in 1874 with J. T. Jones as teacher and was to serve as the provincial school for the Cariboo, Kamloops, Yale and Lillooet districts. About 50 to 60 children attended the school, which was built in about the center of a lot owned by Ashcroft School District 30. In 1880 it was discontinued as a government institution and was operated as a day school, the principal taking in boarders as in a private school.

In the early 1880's Cache Creek was a transfer point for goods brought over the Cariboo road from Yale where mule pack trains were loaded from wagons. Pack trains plied to Savona where small boats and stern-wheelers left for Seymour Arm at the northeasterly end of Shuswap Lake. From there mule trains once again were loaded to carry the goods along trails leading over the Gold Range, a trail cut in 1865 by Walter Moberly, to reach the Big Bend goldfields.

 DRY INTERIOR ZONE This biotic or life zone covers the Okanagan and Similkameen valleys and extends up to Clinton and west to Lytton. It is in this zone that you are now travelling. The elevation ranges from 1000 feet to 3000 and the average rainfall is 15 inches.

In much of the area around Cache Creek and Ashcroft, grasses and trees are scarce, with only sage and rabbit bush covering the ground. Around the fringes we find Ponderosa pine and some Douglas fir, but there is little forest undergrowth. This was not always the case.

When our forefathers came here this area was one of sagebrush and bunchgrass, in which bunchgrass was extremely dominant and sagebrush an occasional species. By turning loose whatever domestic stock they could, the early ranchers virtually wiped out the stands of bunchgrass. Sagebrush and rabbit bush, because of their low palatability, were able to survive and found an environment in which they could increase and dominate. Other weedy species also found a favorable habitat because they did not serve as forage, and thus cheat grass, needle-and-thread grass and cactus also flourished.

CACTUS The cactus you will find here is *Opuntia fragilus,* a small wrinkled plant common to most arid areas. In June and July they blossom with a delicate yellow flower.

CHEAT GRASS *Bromus tectorum* One of the easiest grasses to identify. Just go for a walk and when you return you will find many tiny spears in your socks and shoes. This is cheat grass or downy chess.

NEEDLE-AND-THREAD GRASS This grass, *Stipa comata,* is similar to cheat grass in that you usually find it in your socks, but it differs in having a long piece of 'thread' attached to it.

RATTLESNAKES The rattler is the only venomous snake in B.C. and is found throughout the Interior Dry Belt. It is not unusual to encounter one in the Cache Creek region.

Contrary to popular belief they cannot strike beyond their own length and will avoid trouble and people wherever possible. It is unlikely that you would be bitten unless you stepped directly on one by accident. Rattlers — in fact all snakes — are for some reason loathsome to many people but they should not be killed as they are important predators of mice and other small rodents. If one is found around a habitation, of course, it may have to be killed, although removal would be much better.

The rattler found in this area is the Pacific Rattlesnake, *Crotalus viridis oreganus.* It grows to a maximum length of five feet but the average is around two and a half feet.

Ashcroft Side Trip

ASHCROFT In early 1883, twenty years after the start of the Cariboo gold rush, the flat on the east bank of the Thompson where Ashcroft now stands was a grain field, with only a ranch house and a granary. All around were large ranches growing grain and near the mouth of the Bonaparte stood the Harper Bros. mill. Originally located in Clinton it had been moved closer to the grain supply. John Craig, a Mr. Barnes and the Harpers then built a new road to connect with the Cariboo highway.

It was this year that Bill Bose arrived with a wagon full of crockery, furniture and whiskey to set up a hotel for Mr. Barnes, part owner of the Butte and New Ranches, across from the mouth of the Bonaparte. Barnes knew that the railway was due through there shortly

The Royal Mail stage leaving Ashcroft about 1905 for Clinton, 150 Mile, Soda Creek and Quesnel. Vancouver City Archives photo.

and that if he built a hotel and sold lots a town would develop on his ranch. In 1884 the first train arrived and the town, named after Ashcroft Manor, really started to roll. A ferry ran across the river, piloted by John McKay, but was replaced by a bridge in 1886. In 1885 the Foster store was built and Tom Kirkpatrick built another in 1886. Ashcroft now superseded Yale as the starting point for wagons and mule trains to the upper Cariboo and it remained the transport gateway until the completion of the Pacific Great Eastern Railway to Lillooet in 1915.

Many of the Chinese — or Celestials as then they were called — who came to search for gold or work as coolies on the railway stayed in Ashcroft to open stores and businesses. Wing Chong Tai started business in 1892 and Loy's general store was opened in 1902. Descendants of some of these Chinese families still reside in Ashcroft.

To return to the Cariboo Highway we take the road back across the bridge and then northwest to where it joins Highway 97 at Boston Flats, named for W. H. 'Boston' Sanford, the first man to settle the area and who later ran a hotel in Cache Creek.

'Boston men' was the name the early pioneers gave to Americans, a term from the Boston Tea-party. Anyone nicknamed "Boston" was sure to come from the States.

MONKEY ROCK   A peculiar rock formation on the east of the highway, best seen when travelling south. It occurs just as you pass through a rock cut a short distance south of the town of Cache Creek. The large hill to the east is Elephant Mountain.

Monkey Rock — Trans Canada Highway south of Cache Creek.

BOSTON FLATS   In 1899 the largest pump in B.C. was operated here by John Shields. Run by power supplied by water wheels the pumps lifted water 2,300 feet at the rate of 9000 gallons per minute. They were operated by the Ashcroft Water and Electric Improvement Co.

SOUTHERLY JUNCTION TO CARIBOO HIGHWAY AND ASHCROFT MANOR   3.7 miles to Ashcroft and then 4.8 miles back from town in a V to a second junction with the main highway 97.3 miles north of the point.

The Ashcroft Manor Indian reserve was established at the same time that the Cornwalls settled as it meant that the natives could be close to a source of employment.

The Ashcroft slide of 1880 can be seen from the winding road leading to town. This slide blocked the Thompson River and backed water upstream to the mouth of the Bonaparte River and Harper's mill. A photo in the Ashcroft museum shows the water at a height halfway up the building.

At one time or another Ashcroft has had four bridges crossing the Thompson, the first being built by the San Francisco Bridge Co., in 1886, then another in 1895, one in 1907 and the present one in 1932.

ASHCROFT MANOR   In 1859 two brothers, Henry Penant Cornwall and Clement Fitzalan Cornwall, came via Pemberton Meadows and Pavilion Mountain into the bunchgrass flats above the Thompson River. After building a cabin for the winter they decided to stay and establish a ranch and roadside stopping place. They named the ranch Ashcroft Manor after the family home in Gloucestershire, England.

In 1862 the brothers set up a lumber mill using Cornwall Creek as a source of power. The water was brought to the site in a 960-foot-long ditch and an additional 90 feet of wooden flume, 3 feet wide and one foot high. The lumber was used to build their own homes, which are still standing, and some was sold to other ranchers and miners. In 1864 Joseph W. Trutch was engaged to survey the Cornwalls' land and they applied for water rights to Cornwall Creek.

Not satisfied with a lumber mill and ranch they then purchased mill stones and from 1862 until the Harpers came in 1870 they carried on the service of a local flour mill.

The Cornwalls were used to the old English sports of hunting and riding and in order to maintain a similar atmosphere in the new colony they imported hunting hounds and an Arabian stallion. However, it was not fox that were driven to earth but coyotes, chased over the miles of bunchgrass flats.

Clement F. Cornwall, one of the brothers, was Lieutenant Governor of B.C. from 1881 until 1886. The Parkers, owners of the present manor, are descendants of the original family.

Mile 3

The Bonaparte Church was constructed in 1894 under the direction of Rev. Father J. M. R. Le Jeune, after whom Lac Le Jeune, south of Kamloops, is named. Its hand-hewn logs, now covered with lumber, are still in excellent condition.

The nearby Bonaparte Ranch was founded by Philip Parke in 1867.

Mile 3.4

Bonaparte River crossing. This river is mentioned by name as early as 1828 in records and is presumed to have got its name directly from Emperor Napoleon.

RABBITBUSH *Chrysothamus nauseosus* This low bush, seldom over two feet in height, is often erroneously referred to as sage. However, sage does not bloom until September, while rabbitbush shows its small yellow flowers from August 15 to September 15. It has numerous finely haired, erect stems which give it a neat, compact appearance.

SAGEBRUSH *Artemisia tridentata* Sagebrush is usually indicative of overuse of a once lush grassland. Much larger than rabbitbush it grows from 2 feet to 5 feet in height and has large, tough branches. The tap root often goes down 10 to 12 feet in search of water. Sage has thin, triple leaves, which combined with its aroma readily distinguish it from the smaller rabbitbush.

Although sage is usually connected with cattle, by such songs as, 'Will there be sagebrush in Heaven?', it is often an invader species brought on by too many cattle in too small an area. The presence of sage then usually results in an increase in deer population as they can utilize the plant for browse. Deer, however, are also an invader or 'weedy' species, driving off the climax species. They are not a sign of good range.

TUMBLEWEED This is another species of plant that like the sage is associated with the 'old West' and cattle empires. However, the tumbleweed you might see in this area came from Russia and rapidly spread over North America. It is also called Russian Thistle, *Salsola kali*. The plant, green in spring with soft, spiney stems, breaks off at the ground in the strong fall winds and is blown across the landscape, usually coming to rest against a fence or barn.

AGATE AND PETRIFIED WOOD Both of these are found in the area around Cache Creek. There is one outcropping on the Perry Ranch, 5 miles east of Cache Creek and another in a rock cut about 6 miles south of the town, where quartz crystals are associated with agate.

Mile 3.7
SIDEHILL GOUGER TRACKS. Tracks circling the hills on the right are made by that mythical beast the sidehill gouger *(sidehillus gougeria canadensis)*! Although seldom seen it is not too difficult to catch one, due to its unusual anatomy. Because of its need to feed on side hills nature has adapted this animal to having legs shorter on one side than the other — how much shorter depends on the locality and the angle of the slope. Therefore, all one has to do to catch one is to travel the opposite way to the gouger. He cannot turn around, but if he does try he will roll down the hill, where an assistant can catch the animal. However, it should be added that although many people will say they have seen this beast, few will lay claim to actually having caught one.

It has been said, by the more scientifically minded, that these tracks were made by cattle and that they are a sign of overgrazing, but then no one believes biologists, anyway.

Mile 4   Stop of Interest

Connecting Barkerville with the outside world, the B.X. stagecoaches served the Cariboo for over 50 years. The terminus was moved from Yale to Ashcroft after the C.P.R. construction destroyed the wagon road through the Fraser Canyon. The red and yellow coaches left Ashcroft at 4 a.m. and, 4 days and 280 miles later, reached the end of the road at Barkerville.

MULLEIN *Verbascum thapsus* The tall green plant growing on the roadsides in quantity is the mullein. It reaches a height of 4 feet, has large olive-green leaves and yellow flowers at the top of a long spike. The dead plants often stand all winter.

In the past it was used to cure colds and lung diseases. Deer and cattle are sometimes seen feeding on the stalks.

INDIANS The Interior Salish inhabited the region from south of the U.S.A. border to somewhere just north of Williams Lake, where the Déné people began. The Rockies were their eastern boundary and the Coast range the western.

American Bittern, or "Thunder-pumper" of the marshes.

This language group was divided into four lesser groups or tribes: the Shuswap, Lillooet, Thompson and Okanagan. Their summer homes were the usual 'teepee' type of dwelling, covered with either skins or mats of bark and small twigs. If neither of these was available then brush was used.

In winter the 'kekuli' or 'keekwillie', a semi-subterranean shelter, was built, using poles formed into a conical shape over a 3-foot deep hole some 30 feet in diameter. Exit was through a hole in the top which was reached via a notched pole.

Warfare was not practiced on a large scale but was confined to small skirmishes, usually over an insult or hunting rights. Hunting and fishing were an important full-time occupation. Many fishing and hunting methods were used, including driving elk off a cliff in wholesale slaughter. One particularly ingenious device used for trapping deer was the pit-trap. This was a narrow pit, 6 or 7 feet deep. The bottom was set with sharpened stakes, and a cover, made of small branches lashed together, was suspended on a central roller. As the deer stepped on this, the cover pivoted, causing the animal to plunge in. It then returned to a closed position. If not rendered inactive by the stakes, the deer were prevented from jumping out from the confined space of the covered pit.

Mile 6

Somewhere in this area was 14 Mile House (Ashcroft mileage), Cole McDonald's stopping place, one mile below Hat Creek House.

Mile 6.9

Carquile cabin or Hat Creek Post, at the southwest corner of the highway junction, is almost gone, slowly sinking into the ground. It was built and run by Donald McLean, a chief trader and later a factor of the Hudson's Bay Company. This small cabin was a trading post for the local Indians and was used for many years.

McLean was by all accounts a brutal and cruel man who ruled with an iron fist. In 1849 he set out with an armed posse to avenge the death of a 'company man' who had been killed in an argument with an Indian. Arriving at that family's home they found the wanted man's uncle, son-in-law, step daughter and her baby. Tlel, the suspected murderer, could not be found so McLean and his men murdered all except the daughter. She was wounded when a musket ball struck the baby's head while she held the child in her arms.

Tlel, according to one account, tried twice to avenge his family's death but didn't know that McLean wore a breast plate, protective armor against an assassin's bullet. However, sometime later the trader was killed by a bullet in the back, where the armour plate didn't cover. The shot was fired by a Chilcotin Indian, supposedly in revenge for the Tlel family massacre 13 years previously.

This heartless, rough Scot sired many sons and daughters by Indian women throughout B.C., several of whom were his wives. His second wife, Sophie, was the mother of the 'McLean Boys', a gang who terrorized the Kamloops area in 1879, killing several settlers. They were hanged in New Westminster on January 31, 1881; theirs is the dubious honor of being the only three brothers to be hanged together in British Columbia.

Mile 7

Highway 12, to the west, loops south 50 miles to Lillooet and joins the Trans-Canada Highway at Lytton in the Fraser Canyon. This route is both scenic and interesting for much of it follows the original Cariboo road. It is described as an alternate at Mile 25.

Hat Creek House, one of the old roadhouses, is located just half a mile down Highway 12. It was owned for many years by Steve Tingley, a crack driver of the stagecoach era and later owner of the company. Behind the roadhouse is the old McLean home, now used as a storehouse and dating back to the gold rush. Here the old road can be seen and followed quite easily as it runs along the west side of the valley at the base of the hills. Since this is private property ask permission before you explore.

Hat Creek House, one of the early roadhouses still standing, is located near the junction of Highways 12 and 97.

HAT CREEK This creek flowing into the Bonaparte was formerly called Rivière aux Chapeaux, and derives its name from an Indian village with a large granite boulder nearby, which had in it several hat-like cavities.

Mile 9.5
Across the valley is the old Maggie Mine, now just a yellow-orange stain on the hillside. The mine was opened in 1885 and yielded around $500,000. Named obviously after a girl, the mine's wealth did not bring happiness to the owner. He died a poor man.

Mile 10.5
FERGUSON CREEK Named after the Fergusons who founded an early ranch near here.

A short distance north of this creek colorless, translucent crystals of prehnite fill fissures up to 4 inches wide and 2 to 3 feet long in peridotite rock, along the east side of the Bonaparte Valley.

18 MILE HOUSE (Ashcroft mileage) was located in the vicinity.

Mule deer buck — often seen by travellers.

Whitetail fawns.

MULE DEER *Odocoileus hemionus*   These large deer are often seen
in the fields along the highways. The best times are at dawn and
dusk and the best places, believe it or not, are the many game
crossings which are marked 'Deer Crossing' or 'Watch for Deer'.

The mule deer is B.C.'s most abundant big game species. Approximately 1½ million are estimated to roam the forests and grasslands
of this province. The mule deer differs from the whitetail deer, found
in the southeastern part of the province, by its large ears and its
forked rather than branched antlers. The antlers of the whitetail all
rise from one main beam whereas on the mule each point forks again.
The mulie is also slightly larger.

If you are trying to photograph deer and they hurriedly take off you
might try a trick which hunters sometimes use. While the deer are in
flight give a shrill whistle, the kind where you put two fingers between
your teeth. Often the deer will stop to see what's up and you will have
time for at least one picture. And if you see a doe sneak cautiously
across the road, don't move. A buck may be just behind her, waiting
to see if the coast is clear.

Eastern kingbird.

Mile 12

Scottie Creek Road. A turnoff to the right (east) takes you onto Scottie Creek road. Four and a half miles along this dirt road is an outcropping of amethyst crystals with banded agate. It is located near a fork in the road, on the south side of Scottie Creek just west of the mouth of Chrome Creek and near the 3000 foot level. Crystals are found all along the walls of caves.

SCOTTIE CREEK   Named for William 'Scotty' Donaldson, an Orkneyman who wore his Scots bonnet in all seasons and ran a Roadhouse on the Bonaparte River. A bit of a tippler, Scotty would often rouse his guests with shouts that he was being robbed and murdered and drive them blanketless into the Cariboo night.

Mile 13.6

20 MILE HOUSE   Another one that took its name from the Ashcroft mileage, it was also called the Mundorf Place, after the pioneer owners. The original house, however, burned in 1942 when sparks from a stove pipe ignited a sulphur fumigating compound being used in the rear portion of the house. Behind the stopping place the original road joins the modern highway.

A turn-off to the east takes you to Loon Lake, 12 miles long and one mile wide. It yields some 35,000 to 40,000 rainbow trout per year. The road is steep and gravel for 17 miles to a government campsite. Watch for lumber trucks and give them the right of way. Fishing is good but the water is reported as unsafe for children to swim in. The lake water is often rather warm for drinking but a spring across the lake will provide cool, fresh water. Six campsites are available at the lake.

A short distance in off the highway is the Loon Creek Trout Hatchery, operated by the B.C. Fish and Wildlife Branch.

Mile 14.4

MAIDEN CREEK   So named because Indian maidens bathed in it. At least, that is one story. A more romantic, though sad, story is told of an Indian maid and a young chief. During the winter this young chief went away on a long hunting trip and left the maiden waiting for their marriage on his return. When spring came the maid was still waiting, watching for her lover by the side of this creek. Finally she saw him, but by his side was another girl, a wife he had taken in a distant tribe. The young Indian maid died of grief and was buried where she had kept her watch. From her breasts grew two little mounds, the twin knolls seen today by the mouth of Maiden Creek where it joins the Bonaparte River.

Lake trout — a popular sport fish.

Mile 21.7
Three-mile or Haunted Lake, on whose banks two murders and two suicides are reported to have taken place.

ROCKHOUNDS   Chalcedony, quartz and opal occur in buffweathered serpentine which outcrops on either side of the Bonaparte River valley in a stretch from south of Cache Creek to Clinton. Chrome garnet *(uvarovite)* has also been found in this rock. When fresh, the serpentine is dark green in color with light green translucent patches.

Mile 23.9
On the west of the highway is the Clinton airstrip, and on the east is Soda Lake, the bed of which is almost pure Epsom salts. At one time it was mined.

The old route of the Cariboo Wagon Road can be seen on the eastern shore.

Mile 25
CLINTON   The road to the left as you enter Clinton and pass the cairn is part of the original Cariboo Road to Lillooet, 49 miles away. This route is described as an alternate beginning following Clinton.

Because of its location at the junction of the Lillooet road and the Yale-Cariboo road, Clinton has gone through a number of name changes. Originally an Indian village called Sprague, it became known as Junction when the first miners passed through. Then in 1861 Tom Marshall and Joe Smith built the first hotel and the name became 47 Mile House. Two years later it was named Clinton, after Henry Pelham Clinton, the Fifth Duke of Newcastle, Colonial Secretary in the British Government.

Now a major supply point for the surrounding area, the town has become the administrative center of the Lillooet District and the home of the century old Clinton Ball. Held every May, this is the oldest established event in the Interior of B.C., having begun in 1863 with tickets selling for $10.00 per couple to begin a library fund. In the old days guests came from a radius of 200 miles for a ball that lasted six days and nights. It was the social event of the year for the Cariboo and Chilcotin country, an opportunity to visit and take a break from their constant struggle with crops and cattle.

Traditionally, the ball was held in the Clinton Hotel that had been built by Smith and Marshall in 1861, the town's oldest building. But in 1958, after a rousing centennial celebration, the hotel was destroyed by fire with a loss of three lives. But the ball didn't stop, it just changed quarters.

Robinson's store, built shortly after the hotel by Uriah Nelson, was sold to F. W. Foster in 1864. Foster also had stores in Ashcroft and Lillooet and was evidently somewhat of a lay doctor according to early accounts. The store is still in operation, now holding claim to being the oldest in town. The second oldest is the old school house, a small building made of local red brick, located at the south end of town. It houses one of the most interesting museums in the South Cariboo and should be a definite stop for any traveller.

In the early days of the Cariboo road Clinton was the site of platform scales and a toll-gate, erected by contractor Gustavus Blin Wright whose contract with the government allowed him to collect tolls for a period of five to seven years in order to recoup some of his construction costs.

And in case you think the spirit of the old West is dead, it was in Clinton, only a few years ago, that a gang of 'bad guys', in this case motorcyclists, rode into town and tried to take over. The resulting melee between the gang and an armed and aroused citizenry left several broken, bloody faces and one motorcyclist shot. Only the intervention, in fine old style, of the Royal Canadian Mounted Police prevented further bloodshed.

There is a story told, illustrating the resourcefulness of Cariboo people, of a young clerk in Clinton who was sent an order for a corset from a lady on a remote ranch. Enclosed was a piece of string to give an exact measurement. However, the largest corset in stock was still too small for the rather ample lady. Being a bright young man it did not take the clerk long to figure out a solution. He cut the string to fit the corset and sent both to the customer. No complaint was ever received.

Somewhere in the hills above town is a well hidden cave where a hermit lived for many years, waiting and dreaming of the day he would find a lost gold mine.

An old freight wagon at the Clinton Museum.

Mile 25 — Clinton. The Clinton Hotel in Clinton, destroyed by fire in 1958. The white gate on the left of the photo is the Cariboo road toll gate. Vancouver City Archives photo.

CARIBOO WAGON ROAD   The original Cariboo road, surveyed in 1861, began at Lillooet, the terminus of the Harrison-Lillooet route. In late 1861 contractor Gustavus Blin Wright completed the forty-seven mile section from Lillooet to Clinton, then Cut-off Valley. In May of 1862 Wright was advertising for 500 men to work on the road from there to Alexandria, a contract which he officially signed August 16, 1862. By the end of July 1863 the road had reached Soda Creek and was completed a short time later. As the road was completed, mile-posts, measured from Lillooet, were placed and it was from these original markers that the early Mile Houses took their names.

The following is the description of the alternate route from Lillooet to Clinton:

Mile 0

LILLOOET   Originally known as Cayoosh Flats, due to the body of a cayuse (Indian pony) being found in the river, Lillooet came by its present name about 1860 and was so named because of its position at the end of the trail from Lillooet Lake to the Fraser.

Lillooet is also the name of an Indian tribe and it is generally equated with a native word meaning "wild onion". Some, however, think it came from the Spanish word for "the end of the trail".

St. Mary's Church, until recently the oldest building in town, was built in 1861 but unfortunately was torn down and replaced a few years ago. It is interesting to note that in most early towns the church was one of the first buildings to be erected. More than a place of worship on Sundays it probably served to remind many of the miners of the things they had left behind in England, Scotland, France, Germany or Ireland.

Across from the church is a cairn built of stones taken from the old placer streams. It marks the start of construction of the first Cariboo road.

In 1863 the population is estimated to have been 15,000. Lillooet was the second largest place north of Frisco. The town boasted 13 saloons and 25 other liquor outlets. When Dr. Cheadle visited in 1863, he described it as follows:

"The town of Lillooet is situated on a grand plateau, one of the terraces of the Fraser, which are here more than ordinarily extensive and well-marked. The place was full of miners, on their way down to Victoria for the winter. Drinking and card-playing went on until long after midnight, amid a constant string of oaths and miners' slang.''

Many of the miners didn't have to go far to make their strike. From Cayoosh Creek, just one mile below town, over 3 million dollars in gold was taken out.

POINTS OF INTEREST   Overlooking the town is the "Hanging Tree", reported to have been used 6 times before the coming of Begbie's law and order in 1858. The victims are buried nearby.

The Harrison Trail, running south from Lillooet, was James Douglas' answer to the problem of how to reach the gold fields without the cost of a road through the awesome Fraser Canyon. He made a deal with the miners which would still make Highway Ministers envious. It was spring and the waters of the Fraser were too high for placer mining, consequently many of the miners were idle. Douglas called a meeting of miners and explained how he proposed to build them a trail to the gold fields. Five hundred of them would be divided into teams of 25 and transplanted without cost to the head of Harrison Lake. From here they would build a trail connecting Harrison to Lillooet Lake, the Birkenhead River, Anderson Lake and then Seton Lake. The men would receive free room and board but no pay and would be required to post a $25 peace bond and work guarantee. This amount would be returned to them in goods at the end of the trail. The miners agreed and on August 5th, 1858 the steamer *Otto* left Victoria for what was to become Port of Douglas at the head of Harrison Lake. By the end of September the trail was complete. In time the lakes had steamers on them and the long portage between Anderson and Seton Lakes was equipped with a horse drawn 'railroad'. The trail was virtually abandoned in 1864 when the road through the Fraser Canyon was completed.

Mile 2.4
After leaving Lillooet on the west bank of the Fraser and crossing to the east we reach the junction of the road south to Lytton in the Fraser Canyon or north to the Cariboo Highway and Clinton.

Stop of Interest Sign
LILLOOET   *Here was the gateway to gold-lined bars of the Fraser and beyond was the lure of Cariboo. Like a magnet it drew thousands of miners on the long Harrison Trail through the Coast Mountains. From this focal point the first Cariboo wagon road was started northward in 1858. The trail-end at Lillooet became Mile 0 on the new road to riches.*

33

LILLOOET FLAT Opposite the townsite is the grave of Jonathan Hoiten Scott who died in October, 1882. At the gravesite a bronze tablet has been erected in honor of this man, the first to grow and process tobacco on the mainland of B.C. During the goldrush he sold his product to the miners.

PARSONVILLE, MARYSVILLE AND FORT BERENS Also on this side of the river are two ghost towns and one abandoned fort. Parsonville was near the present day B.C. Hydro pumping station and was thriving in 1863. Marysville was a few hundred yards upstream and Fort Berens just below Parsonville. Fort Berens lasted only a few months, being dependent on Fort Kamloops, and closed before it had really begun.

Two other ghost towns are in this general area, Bridge River and Minto. Bridge River has disappeared and Minto lies beneath 25 feet of water in Carpenter Lake. Those who are interested in ghost towns should obtain a copy of Bruce Ramsey's excellent work, 'Ghost Towns of B.C.', published by Mitchell Press.

Mile 3.1

 Mr. Chernault's farm lies ½ mile down this side road. His farm is well known because of the ice caves which formed when he dug a 36-foot tunnel into the mountain some 28 years ago. Every summer the cave becomes a mass of icicles. One explanation is that the cave is the lower limit of a glacier, another that it is the site of large blocks of ice brought down by a former glacier.

Mile 6

 Viewpoint. From this point you can see the junction of the Fraser and Bridge Rivers and the P.G.E. tracks. The rough foaming water of the Fraser gave the name 'In-hoy-shtin' to the area. It is an Indian name meaning 'Place of Foam'. On both sides of the river are old drying racks and fishing grounds, used for centuries by the Lillooets.

 On the west bank of the Fraser and the north bank of the Bridge River is an old Indian village, which until 1970 was the site of St. James Church. It burned to the ground leaving only a few old cabins and the cemetery, which lies closer to the river. This area can be reached by taking the Bridge River road out of Lillooet.

The name Bridge River comes from a bridge which the Indians had built across the river at this point some years before the arrival of the white man.

Mile 10
Side road to Fountain Valley and Three Lake Valley. The three lakes are Kwotlememo, Chilhil and Cinquefoil. Kwotlememo is also known as Fountain Lake, a good fly fishing lake with large Kamloops trout.

Mile 15
15 MILE HOUSE This important mile house was the first staging place after leaving Lillooet. When last seen these buildings were still in fair condition.

Mile 21.7
PAVILION GENERAL STORE The word pavilion is French for flag or standard and presumably the area got its name because the grave of Te-empt, principal chief of the Shuswaps, placed on a mound at the foot of the mountain, was formerly decorated with many flags.

Mile 22.8
22 MILE HOUSE location. This church and small Indian reserve is the site of 22 Mile House. Extra horses were stabled here for the hard three-mile pull up Pavilion Mountain to the Carson Ranch. From there to 29 Mile is comparatively level.

Here the road forks and the main Cariboo road of 1861 heads over Pavilion Mountain to Clinton. *Our mileage follows this route but Highway 12 to Highway 97 is listed below as a side trip. Take the right branch. Mileage continues.*

Mile 30.6
Pavilion Lake pictograph. This site is marked by a road sign and is situated in Marble Canyon, 150 feet north of Highway 12 and Pavilion Lake. It is 6.6 miles northwest on Highway 12 from the Hat Creek junction and 7.6 miles from the Pavilion railway station. John Corner in his book of B.C.'s pictographs says that the late Bob Selqua, one-time chief of Pavilion Indian village, was reported as saying that his ancestors made these pictographs and that every time a chief died his son painted the picture of a man on the rock. The figures and stars around one such figure indicate his greatness.

Unfortunately, although it is illegal to damage any archeological site, there has been considerable vandalism here.

Mile 31.4
PAVILION LAKE

Mile 32.7
MARBLE CANYON CAMPSITE Situated on Crown Lake this campsite provided 8 campsites and has drinking water available.

Mile 34

Pictograph. Located 3.4 miles east of previous site. The trail to this site begins near an old log cabin in the field on the north side of Highway 12. The site is approximately ½ mile up the trail which follows a steep, rocky draw. One of the finest sites in the Interior, these pictographs are scattered along the cliff for 150 feet. There is a cave above the main panel. The drawings are varied with geometric designs and quadrupeds (bighorn sheep) predominating.

Mile 37.2

Side road to Upper Hat Creek Valley. The road heads south and then follows Oregon Jack Creek east to rejoin Highway 97 south of Ashcroft. The extensive Hat Creek coal deposits are in this region and an attractive outcropping of jasper-agate occurs along a ridge northeast of Upper Hat Creek Village.

Mile 37.2. A freight wagon on the Cariboo road about 1905 or 1906. Note the wheel block dragging behind the rear wheel. Vancouver City Archives photo.

Mile 50.5

Junction of Highways 12 and 97. See Mile 7 on Highway 97 for further information.

The mileage and route now resume at the Pavilion Mountain junction, Mile 22.8.

Mile 26.5

Just as you top a rise, after climbing up out of Pavilion valley, you will come to one of the most beautiful views in British Columbia. Resting in a sea of grass, on a park-like hill dotted with clumps of aspen and pine, is the old Carson ranch.

It had its beginning in 1858 when a young man by the name of Corson left Ohio on a wagon train, bound for the Oregon coast. But Corson never completed the journey. Somewhere along the way he changed his mind and headed for the Cariboo goldfields. He didn't reach them, either. In the hills above the old trail he found a land of grass — grass that was perfect for cattle and horses. He started a string of horses packing between the various miners' camps and finding that the miners couldn't remember his name he changed it to Carson. This was the man who took a cattle drive down the Harrison Trail to what was then Gastown, and now Vancouver. And it was on this same trip that he met his wife and took her back to his castle and kingdom high above Marble Canyon.

Carson died in 1911, and his wife a few years later, leaving several children. Mr. and Mrs. Carson are buried on the ranch. He would have been proud to have seen his son Robert become the speaker of the B.C. Legislature and his youngest son, Ernest, become the Provincial Minister of Public Works. During the latter's term of office, B.C.'s road system was improved to something the old gentleman wouldn't have believed possible.

Mile 30

29 MILE HOUSE on Pavilion Mountain. Only a few scattered ruins remain to mark the location of this second staging place. Extra teams were stabled here for the last hard pull to the summit. Usually these staging places were approximately 15 miles apart.

MILK RANCH   On the lower slope of 6877 foot Mount Carson flows Milk Ranch Creek, emptying its waters into Pavilion Creek near Marble Canyon. The creek takes its name from the so called Milk Ranch which is said to have provided the neighbourhood, miners and travellers with dairy products on their way to the gold fields. Although it was probably the first dairy operation in the province there is no known record of who owned or operated the ranch.

Mile 32

Summit of Pavilion Mountain, 5460. A forestry access road heads west at the summit.

Mile 35

Junction to Arden Park.

Mile 36

Kelly Lake, elevation 3503. Several rough campsites are available around the lake shore.

Mile 36.5

Junction of the road north to Jesmond, Big Bar Lake and the alternate route to Williams Lake. See Highway 97 mileage 31.3.

The nearby Kelly Lake is named after Edward Kelly, who preempted land for the beginnings of the great Kelly Ranch here in 1866.

From here the road follows the course of Cut-off Creek as it flows toward the Bonaparte.

Mile 46

THE TR RANCH, formerly the Spanish or Juan Ranch, established before the gold rush it served as a relay station for pack mules, was started by one of Cataline's packers. Cataline, born in Oleron, Bearn, in what is now part of France, as Jean Jacques Caux, came to the Cariboo in the early 1860's and with Henry Castillou started packing to the various camps. Cataline was the best packer in British Columbia and probably the best in North America. He was one of the Cariboo's characters and many stories are told of him. For instance it was said he always wore a boiled white shirt, replacing it at the beginning of each trip. And it has been reported, depending on the source, that either rum or cognac was his favorite drink, although he was not known as a fussy drinker. His usual procedure was to take a drink and then pour some on his hair, no one is sure why.

When the Cariboo became too settled and crowded for him he moved to the Hazelton area where he continued packing for many years. Finally in the spring of 1922 Cataline took sick and a few weeks later died. He is buried in an unmarked grave overlooking Hazelton.

Log driving on the Quesnel River.

Mile 49

CLINTON *and the junction with Highway 97 where we resume our mileage from Cache Creek.*

Mile 26

A side road to the right leads to Pollard's Guest Ranch, located in 1864 as the Cornish Ranch by John Pollard and John Buxton. It is still operated by members of the Pollard family.

Clinton Creek, which the ranch road follows, is the site of an early flour mill erected by Thaddeus Harper (see Gang Ranch), pioneer of the cattle industry in the Cariboo-Chilcotin. The milled flour was shipped to the gold mining camps by mule. In 1870 the mill was moved to the mouth of the Bonaparte River, just outside Ashcroft, so as to be closer to the grain growers.

Mile 27

Here the road traverses Stawnick Ridge, named after an old Indian woman who, seated on her pony on the ridge, shrieked curses upon members of a police posse who were searching for and eventually captured, her sons, Moses, Paul and Paul Spintlim. The youths were at that time referred to as 'The Outlaws of the Cariboo'. They had been charged with the murder of a Chinese and a teamster. During the 18-month chase, a Corporal Kindness of the B.C. Provincial Police was killed. And, whether or not due to the old woman's curses, five other members of the posse died shortly thereafter!

BIRDS The Cariboo traveller will see many types of birds while travelling the highways and byways. One which you may already have noticed is the Magpie, a large black and white bird with long tail feathers. They are often seen in groups and usually feed on carrion or road-kills. If a flock is seen to fly up from the side of the road as you drive by chances are you will find a dead animal there — a road-kill, or, if it happens to be spring, a winter death.

Another common sight is the undulating flight of the red-shafted flicker. His white back, or tail patch, shows up vividly as he flies just ahead and beside your car. As one of the picidae family of flickers, woodpeckers and sapsuckers, the flicker nests in holes in trees and feeds on grubs and ants.

When winter is beginning to melt in the early warm days of spring the numerous lakes and pot-holes are frequented by migrating swans. Flocks of up to 50 or 60 can be seen resting and feeding. Although not as rare as the trumpeter swans they are protected by law at all times.

Ruffed grouse.

Mile 30.8
P.G.E. underpass.

Mile 31.3
A side road to the west leads to Big Bar Lake, Jesmond and Big Bar Creek, so named for a bog sand bar in the Fraser at the confluence. Just west of Big Bar Lake you may fork north and join up with the main Chilcotin road to Gang Ranch described as Mile 35.9. If you continue to Jesmond you can fork south and join the Lillooet to Clinton road near Kelly Lake.

A reaction ferry is located on the Fraser at Big Bar Creek but the roads on the west bank of the Fraser are rather primitive. These back roads are favorites of car rallies, so don't be surprised if you happen to run into a pack of fast moving little cars with numbers on them.

Big Bar Lake is the former home of Harry Marriott, author of "Cariboo Cowboy". He operated a number of ranches and then consolidated them as O.K. Ranching Co., one of the largest spreads in the area. A cousin of Eric Collier, author of "Three Against the Wilderness", Harry died in 1969, leaving his wife Peg and son Ronald at Big Bar Lake.

Mile 31.4
The end of your long climb up out of the Bonaparte valley. A viewpoint and turnoff on your right offer a good view of the Bonaparte country to the southeast and the Thompson plateau to the east.

You are leaving the Dry Interior Zone and entering the Cariboo Parklands Zone, an area extending from Clinton north to 15 miles south of Quesnel, west to the sloping rise of the Coast Range and east to the North Thompson drainage. The Cariboo plateau does not vary appreciably in elevation, but has more severe weather conditions than the Dry Interior Zone. You have left the Ponderosa pine behind for the Lodgepole pine. Trembling aspen will be seen more frequently, while bunchgrass, sage and rabbitbush are disappearing.

INDIAN PAINTBRUSH This colorful, attractive flower is one that you are likely to see in the Cariboo Parklands. There are many species throughout the province, each having a slightly different shade of yellow, orange or red. The actual flower is hidden by leaf-like bracts which give the plant the appearance of having been dipped in a pot of paint. They grow from 6 inches to 2 feet in height and usually favor shady areas, although yellow paintbrush is sometimes found above timberline in open areas.

Mile 31.5

For a short stretch along the highway here you may notice patches in the telephone poles. It seems that woodpeckers took a particular liking to these nice, smooth trees.

Mile 34

A 3½-mile side road to Painted Chasm, a box canyon 1000 feet deep at its southern end and about one-quarter of a mile wide. The sheer walls are a blaze of color from the exposure to the weather of mineral filled rocks. At the head of the gorge amygdaloidal olivine basalts are exposed in a section over 200 feet thick. The amygdules contain chabazite, heulandite, analcite and opal and are most plentiful near the top of the section.

Local storytellers say that the chasm was formed during the gold rush when a Scot lost a penny and started to dig for it. Lone Butte, 60 miles north, is said to be the pile of earth left from a similar operation.

This road is part of the original Cariboo road and some of the early stage-drivers thought the 'Chasm' was an ideal place for a holdup and the bottom of it a good place for a body. The road loops around the head of the canyon and rejoins the highway at Mile 39.4.

QUARTER HORSES   Cattle country like the Cariboo and Chilcotin means horse country, for where there are cattle there will also be the horse and cowboy.

By far the most popular is what is called the 'Quarter-horse'. Although this horse tends to be a little smaller than some other breeds of riding horses it is indeed a full horse and not just a piece of one! The term came into being because the animal was bred to excel in the running of a quarter mile race. Its ability to run short distances quickly makes it a valuable cow pony.

Mile 35.9

This road to the west leads to some of the Chilcotin country's largest ranches and most spectacular scenery. The 125-mile route is an alternate way to reach Williams Lake. At last check there was only one place to obtain gasoline or supplies — Dog Creek. So travellers should be prepared as they would be for any back road. For the traveller going both ways to Williams Lake it is a fascinating side trip, but best in good weather. A few of the major points of interest are mentioned below.

The Chilcotin country has been described by one writer as a state of mind. But a more accurate description for one who hasn't been there is that the area comprises the drainages of the Chilcotin River. This river takes its name from an Indian tribe and means the people of the Chilco. "Ko" is the native word for water or stream and Chilco has been translated as "warm water" or "young man's river". The river and its people were mentioned by Simon Fraser in his journey down the Fraser in 1808.

Actually, the Chilcotin is one of B.C.'s last frontiers — sprawling cattle country where people wear big hats, riding boots and saddle-worn blue jeans. Recently the cattle ranches have been turning more and more to the tourist trade and it is one of the best and most popular areas for working dude ranches. It is also the home of North America's largest ranches, like the Gang Ranch, Chilco, Alkali Lake Ranch, B.C. Cattle Co., Empire Valley Ranch and many other smaller and not so small spreads.

The Fraser, north of its junction with the Chilcotin.

The road heads west, passing Beaver Lake and a side road north to Dog Creek. You are aware of Meadow Lake, White Lake and Long Lake as you travel through rolling hills of bunchgrass. Another junction, this one heads south to Jesmond and eventually joins the original Cariboo road at Kelly Lake and Cut-off Valley. Continue straight ahead for Dog Creek. Just before you drop into the valley of the Fraser you pass the B.C. Cattle Co. Ranch and Canoe Creek Indian Reserve. Often in this country you will notice that small Indian villages are located close to ranches where work is available for the Indian men as cowboys.

A small deserted homestead in the Alkali Lake area.

An excellent view and photographic point is just beyond the ranch as the road begins its descent to the Fraser River. Across the Fraser can be seen the lands of the Empire Valley Ranch and Gang Ranch.

Gang Ranch and more remote parts of the Chilcotin plateau can be reached by branching at the junction where the suspension bridge crosses the Fraser. Crossing the bridge and driving through the ranch will lead you 25 miles to the Forestry road south of Farwell Canyon. The Forestry road begins at Riske Creek, 35 miles west of Williams Lake and leads beyond Big Creek to the Coast Mountains.

GANG RANCH, largest in North America, is so named because it was here that Jerome and Thaddeus Harper introduced the first gang plough used in the Interior. The nucleus of the ranch was started in the early 1860's.

Jerome and Thaddeus Harper were two brothers who opened up much of the present cattle country in the Cariboo and Chilcotin. They were born in Virginia and worked their way west and north to the Cariboo. In 1861 they started purchasing land in the Kamloops area and when they sold the holdings in 1888 to the Western Canada Ranching Co. they had some 38,572 acres. In Cache Creek they purchased what is now the Perry Ranch, then the original Kelly Ranch near Clinton and in 1883-1885 the property now comprising the Gang Ranch was purchased from the government.

Jerome started importing cattle, buying beef in Washington and Oregon and driving them to the gold fields. As the gold declined so did their business. Jerome died in San Francisco in 1874.

During this time the brothers had bought land near Horsefly, called Harper's Camp, which was later purchased by R. T. Ward, a former 150 Mile storekeeper.

Thaddeus carried on the business, even taking a cattle drive to Chicago but in 1898 he received a serious injury in a riding accident and never recovered, dying in Victoria Dec. 9, 1898.

In 1920 Harpers' Camp changed its name to Horsefly.

DOG CREEK HOUSE   Built in 1856 by Raphael Valensuela and operated for many years by J. S. Place, it was advertised as 'Dog Creek Hotel' and boasted of having "first class stabling, headquarters for the Dog Creek stage line, the finest wines, liquors and cigars. Good table and attendance".

On the mountain above there are still signs of five graves which tell a tale of tragic love in the 1880's. The graves contain the remains of five Indian maidens who all fell in love with the same white man. Each thought she was his only love, until the day came when they discovered he was 'playing fast and loose' with all their affections.

Each took a rope and rode up the mountain and there the bodies were found the next day, hanging from the same fir tree. The tree still stands overlooking the five graves.

A pictograph and cave can be found near here, ½ mile north of the road at the base of a basaltic cliff facing south. The red ochre pictographs are at the back of a spectacular cavern, 210 feet wide, 50 feet deep and 10 feet high at the entrance. The cliffs are visible from the settlement of Dog Creek. To find them, walk along the base of the cliffs in an easterly direction, keeping a close watch as the entrance is obscured by shrubs and brush. Teit, in his early journals, says that Indian youths used the cave for sleeping, praying and dancing during training. He interprets the drawings as ruffled grouse, fir branches and people. The floor of the cavern is covered with many feet of silt.

SOOPOLALLIE *Shepherdia canadensis* These bright red berries grow on bushes 3 to 4 feet in height and when mixed or beaten form a froth not unlike whipped-cream. This is how they came by their Indian name (soop-soap: olallie-berry). The leaves are roughly egg-shaped and grow opposite each other with the berries forming clumps. The twigs are pebbly with rust and the fruit is almost transparent.

It is still not uncommon to find Indian children in the more remote areas eating a bowl of these berries. The most common way, and the original method, was to use a very flexible wooden spoon to whip the berries into a froth. They are not, however, particularly sweet and if you try them you will probably prefer them with a sprinkling of sugar.

ALKALI LAKE RANCH Appears to hold the claim of being the first cattle ranch in B.C. The first pre-emptor was Herman O. Bowe on March 19, 1861 with a partner Philip Grinder, who later abandoned his right. Bowe recorded 320 acres in his own name Sept. 7, 1867. As well as operating a ranch here he opened a wayside stop for travellers on the early trails and roads of this region.

ALKALI LAKE A particularly good spot to look for migrant casual bird visitors. During the last few years such strange visitors as the following have been recorded here:

Common Eider: accidental in 1950
Gyrfalcon: rare winter visitor in November and January
Ring-necked pheasant: introduced
Whooping crane: accidental in 1967
Long-billed curlew: breeds in B.C. but only in scattered locations
Pomarine jaeger: accidental in 1911 and 1967.
Band-tailed pigeon: casual visitor, seen in 1967
Burrowing owl: casual visitor, seen in 1949
Lewis woodpecker: a scarce breeder
Bobolink: a rare breeder, seen in 1959
Bullock oriole: a scarce Cariboo breeder, but regular here
Lark Bunting: casual visitor, seen in 1969
White pelican: uncommon in B.C. but regular here during migration

If you are interested in birding and find any nests, make a note of the position, location, date, contents and species and drop a note to the Pacific Nest Records Scheme, c/o Mrs. L. A. Gibberd, 465 Ellis St., Penticton, B.C. Mrs. Gibberd will send you cards to fill out with the appropriate information if you wish. In a scheme such as this, amateurs can contribute greatly, as they are in the field so much and almost everyone finds a bird's nest in the spring.

WHITE PELICANS Often seen on Alkali Lake during the spring and fall migrations. They are a rather unique bird in British Columbia for there is only one known breeding colony west of the Canadian Rockies. It lies at Stum Lake, some 22 miles northeast of Alexis Creek.

A few years ago pelicans in B.C. were in danger due to disturbance of their nesting sites and because of pesticides. After a public protest the B.C. Fish and Wildlife Branch closed the lake during the breeding season to allow the birds to nest undisturbed.

In April, 1971 the Department of Recreation and Conservation under The Hon. W. K. Kiernan formed the 3,082-acre White Pelican Provincial Park, for the express purpose of protecting the birds. No motors are allowed on the lake and visitors must keep well away from the breeding islands. A park naturalist is resident during the summer months, but tourists are not encouraged due to the possibility of disturbing the birds. The lake is closed to trespass from Mar. 1 to Aug. 31 each year.

The other problem affecting the pelicans is pesticides such as DDT. This poison is found in fish which have become infected due to aerial spraying and agriculture run-off water. Fish are the main food supply of pelicans and the pesticides result not only in poison-

White pelicans in flight.

ing the bird slowly but in a high percentage of egg breakage in the nesting colony. Whether or not pelicans, along with many other birds, can survive this problem, only time will tell.

Pelicans are easy to identify. They are birds weighing about 18 pounds with a wingspread of 8 to 9 feet. They are pure white with distinctive black wingtips and in breeding have a horny protuberance on the upper bill. They feed on fish, usually working in groups to drive the small fry into shallow waters along lake shores, where they can be easily scooped up in their large, pouch-like bills. Nesting on islands they have few predators except gulls and man and in B.C. they have recently been given protection by being classed as gamebirds with a closed season all year.

 SPRINGHOUSE RANCH   12 miles from Williams Lake. A short distance north of this ranch we come to the Chimney Creek crossing and a junction. The right fork heads to Chimney Lake where sandhill cranes are sometimes seen in the spring. It is thought that they nest in the marshes at the end of the lake. On the west side of the lake an osprey usually nests, high in a broken snag. The creek and lake get their name from a chimney-like butte at the mouth of the creek.

The old Springhouse school, now a community hall, on the open meadows of the Chilcotin.

 PINCHBECK RANCH   This ranch is on your right as we continue. It was established in 1862 by Mrs. Matilda Pinchbeck's father, Amadee Isnardy. A few miles from here we come to the junction of the Dog Creek road and the Williams Lake to Bella Coola road. Only a mile away is the town of Williams Lake. *Our mileage now resumes on Highway 97 north of Clinton.*

Great horned owl, one of the larger owls found in the Cariboo.

A single file of white pelicans cruise a lake in search of food.

Mile 37.2

59 MILE HOUSE   The original roadhouse burned down in 1946. The twelve-mile stretch which you have just travelled from Clinton, probably in about 12 minutes, used to take freight wagons one full day.

EYES   What beast is that whose eyes shine in the night? Well, if it is not the bottom of a beer can or pop bottle reflecting your headlights and if you can see the color you might be able to identify it. The raccoon's light is yellow, the otter's amber, the coyote's golden — as are some bears — and the bobcat's is green. Some of the reptiles' eyes have an orange glow.

Mile 39.4

The Ponderosa pine which was common in the drier regions has now given way to the Lodgepole pine, *Pinus contorta*. Found over most of B.C. it is one of the most valuable timber trees in Canada, being used for railway ties, timbers and poles and in the manufacture of pulp. The tall, slender tree arrives at its name due to the uniform diameter over its 50 to 100 foot height and the fact that native Indians used it for building their lodges.

Although not a timber-line species, the Lodgepole grows at an altitude of 2000 to 6000 feet and thrives in deep, moist, well-drained loam, growing in even-aged stands with Douglas fir and Engelmann spruce.

Small lakes and pot-holes of the Cariboo plateau are full of a great variety of bird life, particularly during the nesting season.

Stands of tules or reeds will hold the woven nests of red-wing and yellow-headed blackbirds. The coot will be building its nest on a floating mass of rotting vegetation, similar to the grebes but often more in the open. The ruddy duck will be found nesting in the reeds close to shore, while the mallards, pintails and teal will be in the grass along the shore. Some mallards and pintails will be found up to a mile from water, depending on where they are obtaining their food.

Although a common migrant species the Canada goose is not a plentiful breeder in this region. Their nests are sometimes found around the lakes or streams, or tucked away in some more remote marsh.

The black tern will be found on some lakes, such as Stum, and is easily identified by its tern shape, dark coloration and its frequent swooping and darting over the waters in search of food.

Two gulls are seen in this area. The herring gull, a large gull generally referred to as the common seagull of the coast, breeds on rocky islets in some lakes. He is large and not easily confused with the Bonaparte's gull which is somewhat rarer, smaller and has a completely black head in a mature specimen.

Loons are also found on the larger lakes, usually one family to a lake, building their nest within easy reach of water and escape, as the position of their legs makes them unbalanced and awkward on land.

CAMELS   In 1862 a packer by the name of Frank Laumeister had what he thought was a fantastic idea. Frank knew that camels could carry more than twice the weight of mules, cover three times the distance in a day and that they had the ability to travel for long distances without food or water. He reasoned therefore that they would be useful for packing on the Cariboo road, so he bought 21 from the U.S. Army, who had been using them for the same purpose.

What Laumeister hadn't figured on was the vicious temperament and potent, strange aroma of the beasts. Strings of mules would go into sheer panic upon meeting a camel train and dash into the bush or over a cliff, scattering packs and packers far and wide.

Two years and countless troubles, lawsuits and petitions by angry packers passed and finally Frank had to give up his brain child. Some of the camels were sold and the remainder were turned loose near Kamloops. Fortunately they didn't breed and multiply or the problems might have continued for years, causing vegetation damage as burros have in parts of the U.S.A. The last one died in 1905 after wandering free for 41 years.

Mile 45.2

70 Mile House, or Boyd's House, burned down in 1956 after oper- ating since 1862. The following history hung on the living room wall:

"The contract for building the Cariboo Road, from Lillooet to Clinton, a distance of 47 miles was granted to the contractors, G. B. Wright and John C. Galbraith, at the rate of $1,709 per mile, and to be built where they saw fit subject to the approval of the government; hence a crooked and hilly road resulted. When this portion of the road was built the same contractors secured the contract to build the road from Clinton to Soda Creek, a distance of 130 miles, at the same rate and privileges as before."

Early in 1862 the road reached the 70 mile post. Here the contractors decided to build a wayside house, thus the "Seventy Mile House" was built and soon became a favorite stopping place. All

A small flock of whistling swans, one of many often seen during spring migrations through the Cariboo.

Mallard duck and drake.

Many hawks such as the sharp-shinned frequent and nest throughout the Cariboo.

An osprey, a declining species, still nests in some parts of the Cariboo.

Damsel flies are just one of many insects that can be found in the marshes and bogs or swamps of Cariboo lakes.

the logs used in the building were hewn by hand from selected trees and extended the entire length of the building.

"Several years ago (1899) the government measured the road from Ashcroft and attempted to change the names of the stopping places but the owners objected, preferring to retain the original historic names. The Cariboo Road was opened to traffic at the end of September, 1863 from Lillooet to Soda Creek, a distance of 266 miles."

 CARIBOO PLATEAU SIDE ROAD This road heads east across the plateau, branching shortly to circle around Green Lake. Just beyond the settlement of North Bonaparte the road again forks to the right and leads through the Bonaparte valley to Bonaparte Lake and eventually to Highway 1 west of Kamloops.

Before reaching Highway 24 at Bridge Lake we find another road branching to the right which passes Egan Lake and joins the Bonaparte road north of Bonaparte Lake.

Highway 24 leaves the Cariboo Highway at Mile 93 and is described at that mileage. A government campsite is located at Bridge Lake and is noted on the Highway 24 section.

 THE FUR BRIGADE TRAIL This is the old Hudson's Bay Company trail leading from Fort Kamloops and points south to Fort Alexandria, Fort St. James and other northern posts. The trail was opened in 1842 and can be traced along the shores of Green Lake.

Green Lake, twenty miles long and two miles wide, was once the scene of trading among the Indian tribes, long before the coming of the first fur traders.

Cattle and a snake fence, typical of many Cariboo scenes.

THE FLYING U RANCH A short distance down this side road is a ranch, pre-empted by J. G. Boyd of 70 Mile House. It was probably used to grow produce for the roadhouse. A penciled note on the pre-emption papers that 'squatter has left the country' indicates that someone had been there before him. Portions of the Fur Brigade Trail can be seen through the long pasture and as many Indians used the area, arrow and spear heads are frequently found. A short distance from No. 1 green on the golf course can be seen the round Keekwillie hole of an Indian dwelling.

TREMBLING ASPEN This tree is one of the more commonly seen varieties in the Cariboo Parklands. A deciduous or broad-leafed tree it can usually be recognized by its trembling or quaking during any slight breeze, and in the autumn by the brilliant gold patches it produces along the lakes and on the rolling hills.

The leaves are 1½ to 3 inches long and are borne on long flattened stems. They are shiny, dark green above and yellowish-green below. The bark is smooth and greenish to yellowish on a young tree, becoming rough, furrowed and grey to brown on a mature specimen.

B.C. What does B.C. stand for? Well, usually it means British Columbia, unless you happen to be discussing dates and then it means 'Before Christ'. Or if you happened to be an English mutineer soldier in the 1800's you might have had 'B.C.' tattooed on your upper arm. It denoted 'Bad Character'.

INDIAN NAMES Indian names often confuse travellers in B.C. into believing that they have two christian names and no surname. For instance, Jimmy Joe or Lennie Bob. The reason is that an Indian boy takes his father's first name and not his last, as is our custom. Thus, if a boy was called Jack and his father's name was Jimmy Bob, he became Jack Jimmy.

Sometimes a name indicated a peculiar physical deformity or size, such as Lame Bob, Big Jimmy, Little Jimmy Lick or Long Johnny.

Mile 48.2
Cunningham Road turns to the west. A short bush road leading past small pot-holes to Cunningham Lake. Named after Cunningham's House or 74 Mile House.

INDIAN LEGEND Once in ancient times, the Crees from the east, the Thompsons from the south and the Lillooets from the west made up their minds to attack the Shuswaps of the north. They

Aspens in the fall.

met on the east bank of the Fraser River and there joined forces. Numbering several hundred men, they advanced up the river to attack the Shuswaps but when nearly opposite the mouth of Lone Cabin Creek and still some distance from Canoe Creek, they were met by Coyote, or some other transformer, who changed them into pillars of clay. They may be seen standing there now — the tall Crees on the right, the Thompsons of medium height in the center and the short Lillooets on the left. (Recorded by J. A. Teit, Publications of the Jessup North Pacific Expedition.)

Mile 48.5

You are now travelling on the 'bonny, bonny banks of Loch Lomond', probably named by some early son of Scotland.

Killdeer — the double black band and ringing "Kill-Deer" voice serve as a ready identification of this common summer resident of B.C. and the Prairie Provinces.

SHOREBIRDS Shorebirds frequent lakes such as this during most of the year, except winter. In early spring they are looking for nesting sites and travelling to the north and the barren grounds. In summer resident nesters like the killdeer are often seen, running ahead of you as you walk along, trying to divert your attention from the young birds hidden nearby. Their cry of 'killdeer, killdeer', their double breast band and white-banded wings mark them well for the bird-watcher.

Bobbing along the shore, looking very unbalanced, is the spotted sandpiper. So named for his very distinctive breeding plumage, a spotted breast, he is constantly in search of small bugs and insects.

ALKALI   The white substance seen on this and other lakes in the Cariboo and Chilcotin is generally called alkali. It forms in areas of low rainfall when salts, leached out from the surrounding hills, are left by evaporating water. A lake which is particularly saturated could become the poison water referred to in so many western novels and movies.

Any lake or flat with the name "Alkali" probably came by it through its appearance or taste.

Mile 56.3
Bullock Lake Road to the west leads 8 miles to 83 Mile Lake and Bullock Lake.

Mile 56.5
83 Mile or Stoddart's House.
1862   The original house was built.
1865   Became the office for the Overland telegraph.
1868   Murdock Ross purchased the house and it became a post for changing horses.
1886   Purchased by the B.X. Company and the barns enlarged to accommodate 50 head of horses.
1901   Stoddart bought the property and buildings.
1923   While owned by Orford and Templeton who had purchased it a few years before, the original house burned to the ground. A few of the log buildings may be seen in the fields just off the highway.

Stages leaving Ashcroft at 4 a.m., the usual time, would reach 83 Mile, under favorable conditions at 6 p.m. The stage left at 4 a.m. the next morning, no matter what time it had arrived the night before, for the mail contract demanded delivery on time. If passengers didn't have time to sleep in the Roadhouse they got what they could aboard the coach.

STAGECOACHES   In the days of the Cariboo wagon road, stages were the main means of passenger transportation. They varied from two horse rigs, used to connect the short runs, to four or six-horse teams for the large Concord stages.

The fare, Ashcroft to Barkerville, was $42.50 in winter and $37.50

A moose feeding on aquatic plants in a Cariboo marsh.

Winter tracks.

A beaver lodge.

A beaver with his food supply.

in summer, with 40 pounds of baggage allowed. The baggage weight sounds very similar to our present day airline restrictions.

Women, no matter what their station in life, were given every courtesy of the road, the best seat in the stage and the best chair in the dining rooms of the Roadhouses. The drivers were picked for their skill as drivers and horsemen, and were always thinking of their passengers' well being. The B. X. Co. took good care of its passengers and of its equipment. The red and yellow stages were always freshly painted and the handmade harness was kept in good repair.

For 50 years they were the kings of the road, but gradually the competition of railways and the newer automobiles put them out of business. The last mail stage ran up the road in October, 1915. No more would the clip-clop of horses' hooves, the jingle of harness, the songs of the drivers and the shouts of the passengers greet the old road. They had all gone to be succeeded by the roar and exhaust of the internal combustion engine.

Mile 58.3

MOUNT BEGBIE FORESTRY LOOKOUT   A rough dirt road to the east leaves the highway at an elevation of 3983 feet and climbs up to 4140 feet and the forestry lookout. The road is rough and not suitable for trailers. The mountain is named after Sir Matthew Begbie, a judge in the days of the gold rush. Although the lookout elevation is not particularly high, a good view is afforded because of the relatively flat Cariboo plateau. The tower is manned from May to September and is used for spotting forest fires started by lightning or careless campers. The forester will probably be glad of a visitor and if asked politely may show you how his sighting device works. If the fire hazard is high, watch your fires and cigarettes, and don't bother the man, he is probably busy.

On the same hill are the micro-wave towers of the B.C. Telephone Co.

Mile 61.6

Davis Lake road to the west. 5 miles to the lake.

OWLS   There are 15 species of owls in B.C., seven of which it is possible to see in the areas you are travelling through. The great grey owl is seen mainly in the north but like the snowy owl he sometimes comes south in the hard winters when food is short in the tundra. The long-eared prefers deciduous woodlands but it is possible you will see him, or the tiny screech owl, a small eared owl. The short-eared is frequently seen on the Lower Mainland of B.C. and can be recognized because of his habit of hunting in the daytime and his 'quartering' of fields during his searching for rodents. The saw-whet is a very small hornless owl who hunts only at night, while the pygmy, the smallest in Canada, is smaller but hunts in the daytime. Finally the great horned owl is also seen in this region and is easily recognized by his size and large feather 'horns'.

Short-eared owl — one of many Cariboo owls.

Each species of owl has a different sound of 'who-who' or 'hoot' and it is said that because of their snoring they have been the cause of many so-called haunted houses, or ghosts in the night. In fact, owls have generally been associated with evil things and beings, perhaps because they are predators and usually fly at night. Actually they are a most important rodent control — far better and safer than traps or poison.

In early spring the Balsam root or sunflower can be seen in the Cache Creek area.

Asters   Showy Daisy   Butter and eggs

Mile 65.5

93 mile service, where a large helpful area map is erected.

BACKROADS Throughout the Cariboo plateau are numerous back-roads, all holding a charm and mystery to the interested, adventurous traveller. Most of these roads are described at the appropriate milepost, but a word of caution. Travel prepared. Sudden rain or snow could make the roads all but impassable, and help, if you're stuck, could be a long time coming. All cars should carry the following:

A good spare tire, or two
A working jack, preferably with a large base
A good shovel, not an entrenching tool
An axe, sharpened so that it will cut properly
Extra water
Tire chains for mud or snow
A tow rope
Extra gas

Always check and fill your gas tank before leaving the highway — for two reasons. You might run out, and it is cheaper.

Mile 66

Highway 24 to Highway 5 and the Cariboo plateau. Described as two separate side trips with the main points of interest. The first portion describes the 55-mile section from 93 Mile to Wells Gray Park and Mahood Lake. The second travels from 93 Mile to Little Fort on Highway 5, north of Kamloops. There are many more junctions and side roads than it is possible to list and it is quite common to become 'confused' as to where you are. Obtain a good map and keep track of the turn-offs you take.

This whole plateau is dotted with many fine fishing lakes offering Kokanee, brook trout, rainbow and lake trout. Most of the larger lakes are best for trolling but a few of the smaller waters and streams offer good fly-fishing.

Cariboo Highway mileage resumes after these side trips.

Mile 5.6

LONE BUTTE A small supply settlement and P.G.E. station for the many local guest ranches. It is named for the large butte to the east.

The community of Lone Butte on Highway 24.
The butte can be seen in the distance.

Mile 12
You are now passing along the southerly shore of Horse Lake, a spot the Indians found particularly good for grazing their horses. Some of the ranches in this area offer pack-trips to remote unspoiled fishing lakes in the quiet areas of the plateau.

Mile 21.1
Another junction with the left going to Wells Gray Park and the right heading to the main Cariboo plateau road.

Murtle River Bridge, Wells Gray Park.

Mile 23.8
Right fork takes you to Deka Lake. Popular for Kamloops trout and char fishing.

Mile 27 to 32
Three lakes are passed in this section of the road — Sulphurous, Hathaway and Drewry.

Mile 44.6
Side road to the left leading to Canim Lake, described 73.1 on the Cariboo Highway.

Mile 51.3
Canim River Falls are only a short 5 to 10 minute walk. The river, draining Canim Lake, offers excellent fly-fishing for rainbow trout. It is about five miles long and flows into Mahood Lake, which is the source of the Mahood River, a tributary of the Clearwater and Thompson system.

Mahood Lake is named for J. A. Mahood who ran a C.P.R. survey along the lake shore in 1872.

Mile 54
From here a new road runs two miles into Wells Gray Park. This is rather a back entrance, however. The main access to the park is from Highway 5 north of Kamloops, giving boat access to Clearwater and Azure Lakes.

The park is named after The Hon. Arthur Wellesley (Wells) Gray, Provincial Minister of Lands in 1933. It is basically a wilderness type of park with little development in the way of tourist facilities and campsites.

The second of the two side trips now starts, with the mileage once again beginning at the Cariboo Highway, and descriptions beginning at the first junction.

Mile 7
Junction. Keep to the right fork for Little Fort.

Mile 7.3
Junction. The right fork heads 29 miles southwest, joining the Cariboo Highway at Mile 45.2 where it is described.

Mile 16.1
2.2-mile side road to Fawn Lake.

Mile 20.2
Another route to Canim Lake.

Mile 25.7
After passing Roe Lake on the left we pass this side route to a couple of the area's guest ranches.

Mile 31.2
Turn left for Highway 5 and right for 70 Mile House.

Mile 32.6
Bridge Lake park and campsite. Thirteen campsites with excellent fishing and swimming. Carry drinking water. Boat launching. This area of the Cariboo plateau is excellent moose habitat and is particularly popular with hunters in the fall.

Mile 32.9
Junction. The left fork circles Bridge Lake and the right leads to Little Fort.

Mile 33.8
Side road to Montana Lake, 7 miles, and 3 miles farther, Machete Lake.

Mile 36.5
The road to Little Fort follows Lac des Roches for several miles, now and then becomes narrower and more winding as it runs through Eakin Creek Valley.

Mile 64.3
Highway 5. LITTLE FORT settlement is just a short distance away. Little Fort is an old Hudson's Bay Company trading post and was mentioned by surveyor A. R. C. Selwyn in his report of 1871-72. " . . . we camped on a fine flat above The Little Fort, an old and now deserted Hudson's Bay Company trading post."

The descriptions now resume at Mile 66.3 on the Cariboo Highway, just north of 93 Mile House.

 ROADHOUSES In 1862-1863 Dr. W. B. Cheadle and Viscount Milton made a trip across Canada to Victoria. From here they travelled up the Harrison Trail to Clinton, then by wagon over the Cariboo Road to Soda Creek. The road was as yet incomplete to the goldfields so from here they took a sternwheeler to Quesnel Mouth and then walked to Richfield and Barkerville. As stages were only beginning to run, the roadhouses were not yet developed the way they would be in later years. A page from the account these two gentlemen wrote after returning to England shows us what the stopping places were like in October, 1863:

"The accommodation along the road was everywhere miserable enough, but after leaving Clinton it became abominable. The only bed was the floor of the 'wayside houses', which occur every ten miles or so, and are named the 'Fiftieth' or 'Hundredth Mile House' according to the number of the nearest milepost. Our solitary blankets formed poor padding against the inequalities of the rough-hewn boards, and equally ineffectual to keep out the cold draughts which whistled under the ill-fitting door of the hut. A wayside house on the road to the mines is merely a rough log hut of a single room; at one end a large open chimney, and at the side a bar counter, behind which are shelves with rows of bottles containing the vilest of alcoholic drink. The miners on their journey up or down, according to the season . . . come dropping in towards evening in twos or threes, divest themselves of the roll of blankets slung upon their backs, and depositing them upon the floor use them as a seat, for the hut possesses few or none. The next thing is to have a 'drink', which is proposed by someone of the party less 'hard up' than his friends, and the rest of the company present are generally invited to join in.

"After supper and pipes, and more 'drinks', each unrolls his blankets, and chooses his bed for the night. Some elect to sleep on the counter, and some on the flour sacks piled at one end of the room, whilst the rest stretch themselves on the floor, with their feet to the fire. Occasionally a few commence gambling, which, with an accompaniment of drinking and blasphemy, goes on for the greatest part of the night."

As can be seen from this account the accommodations were anything but luxurious, and not up to the standards which later came to be expected of the road and its stopping places.

DEATH CAMAS *Zygadenus venenosus*   Death camas is very similar to the camas plant that grows in the Gulf Islands region of B.C. The several long thin leaves have a groove on one side which forms a keel on the underside. These leaves, when young, can prove fatal to grazing stock. The bulb of the death camas is highly poisonous and was sometimes used by the natives in the same way hemlock was used by the Romans. The easiest way to distinguish the two plants is the yellow flower on the death camas and the blue on the camas.

Mile 69

98 MILE HOUSE Near here, in July, 1892 a B. X. stage was held up and robbed of $15,000 from the Barkerville goldfields. News spread fast but although many posses searched the Bonaparte country they found only an empty strongbox.

Later that same year a man named Sam or Jack Rowlands struck gold on Scottie Creek. The peculiar thing about it was that although many other miners were trying their luck only Rowlands found gold. Suspicions were aroused and the B.C. Provincial Police began to watch Sam and his gold. When he announced that "the gold had played out and he was moving on", the Chief Constable arrested him. In short order he was tried and found guilty of the 98 Mile stage robbery and sentenced to five years in the B.C. Penitentiary. At the age of 62, after serving two years of his term, he escaped and disappeared.

Only $3,000 in gold had been recovered and many thought he would return to Scottie Creek to retrieve the rest, but Sam and his gold were never seen again. Perhaps it is still there, hidden somewhere along the banks of Scottie Creek.

Despite the prevailing stories of the few robberies in the Cariboo and the reluctance of some to hire guards, 'because there was no danger', not everyone felt that way. Our friends Cheadle and Milton describe one party they met in 1863.

"On the road we met a small bullock wagon, escorted by twenty armed miners on foot. This proved to contain 630 pounds weight of gold, the profits of a Mr. Cameron, the principal shareholder in the noted Cameron claim. This gold, worth about 30,000 pounds sterling, had been amassed in the short space of three months and represented probably less than one-half the actual produce of the mine during that time."

Mile 69.5

P.G.E. OVERPASS. The Pacific Great Eastern Railway (recently re-named the British Columbia Railway) had its beginning in 1912 when a group of private contractors offered to build a new railway for British Columbia. Their plan was to start at North Vancouver, travel west along the shore, then into the hills and through them to the Squamish valley. From here the line would extend up the Interior to Quesnel and then to Prince George. The idea was to connect with the Grand Trunk Railway and provide that system with an access to Vancouver.

Unfortunately for the promoters, soon after construction was begun the Grand Trunk and Canadian Northern were merged to form the

Canadian National, operated by the Canadian government. This meant they had a route to the coast and the P.G.E. promoters went broke.

The provincial government attempted to complete the half-finished railway but failed and finally closed the Vancouver to Squamish section. B.C. now had a railway from Squamish to Quesnel. In spite of many promises at election time, it was not completed for many years. It remained a railway that started nowhere and went nowhere.

Finally in 1958 the first engine reached the banks of Peace River. The railway had been completed by the provincial government as a Centennial gift for the people of the North. The P.G.E. was at last complete, although extensions are still being built.

Bruce Ramsey has written a book entitled *P.G.E. Railway to the North,* published by Mitchell Press in 1963, for those who wish more detailed information on the many political ramifications that seem to be a necessary part of any railway.

Mile 71.6

100 MILE HOUSE   Originally known as Bridge Creek this was a resting place for the fur brigades. Tom Miller first built here in 1862-65, followed by Nelson and Charlton in 1874. In 1877 a Telegraph office, later moved to 115 Mile, opened here. In the middle 1880's Thomas Hamilton, one of a large pioneer family living at 114 Mile Ranch,

100 Mile House about 1898. The Royal Mail Stage has stopped for a few moments while horses are changed or a meal eaten. Vancouver City Archives photo.

operated the stopping place, selling to William Allen. Then came the Stephenson brothers who in 1912 sold to the Marquis of Exeter. By this time the original holdings had grown to 12,000 acres. For a time the Marquis ran the Bridge Creek Ranch from his home in England and then in 1930 his son, Lord Martin Cecil, came to B.C. and took over operation of the estate. He proceeded to build a new lodge and stopping place, which was only just complete, when in 1937 the original structure went up in flames.

Although 100 Mile had its beginning as a stopping place and cattle ranch the lumber industry was really responsible for the growth of the town. At this time the town land was under the control of Bridge Creek Estates and the town remained unincorporated so that Lord Martin Cecil and his directors could control construction and be sure no tar-paper shacks were put up.

100 Mile is now a thriving lumber community on the Cariboo plateau, capable of meeting all the needs of tourists.

What is supposed to be the oldest building in the region is located at the rear of 100 Mile Lodge. It is not known precisely when the building was constructed but for many years it was a carpenter's shop, which probably accounts for its fine construction. Now the building serves as a chapel for the Emissaries of Divine Light, a religious order whose Canadian headquarters are located at 100 Mile under Lord Martin. Visitors are welcome to inspect and visit the old building.

Mile 72.5

At the top of the hill out of 100 Mile we reach the junction of the road to Canim Lake.

The following is a side trip with the main points of interest mentioned.

Mile 7.4

The road follows Bridge Creek, which empties many of the lakes in this area.

Mile 9.5

BUFFALO CREEK POST OFFICE and side road to Buffalo Lake.

Mile 13.2

At the small community of Forest Grove the road divides and makes a 25-mile loop, touching the end of Canim Lake and returning to Forest Grove. The right fork is the shortest to the lake and the government campsites. Our mileage follows this route.

CHINOOK   A jargon used throughout the northwest as a trade

language. It appears to have been in use to a limited degree prior to 1800 but it was the Hudson's Bay Company that really developed the language. The words came from Indian tongues, English, French and American and took on similarities to all of these. A few words, such as 'tic-tic' for watch or clock, were formed by onomatopoeia. Because the jargon only had a rather limited number of words, several hundred, the user had to become adept in the coupling of words into groups to make himself more versatile in conversing. A few of the words are still familiar today. Such as Mowitch — deer, Cultus — bad, Cheechako — newcomer or tenderfoot, Skookum — big, strong.

Mile 26.4
CANIM BEACH PROVINCIAL PARK 14 campsites and drinking water available. Canim is the Chinook word for canoe.

Mile 29.5
The road now loops back and heads west for 22 miles to Forest Grove, passing Hawkins and Ruth Lakes. A forestry access road continues on through Horsefly to the Cariboo Highway. Turn across Eagle Creek.

Mile 51.5
HENDRIX LAKE townsite for the Boss Mountain molybdenum mine. The town is named after Slim Hendrix who lived at the foot of Canim Lake and ran a trapline in the area of Hendrix Creek. He died in 1938.

There are no tourist accommodations here but food, gas and restaurant meals are available. The mine and 1000-tons-a-day concentrator are six miles away. The ore was first discovered in 1911 but active development didn't occur until Noranda Exploration optioned the property in 1961.

Mile 52-67.5
From here we pass Bosk Lake, noted for its rainbow; Crooked Lake, where ospreys nest; and then reach the Horsefly River and bridge. We follow the Horsefly River.

Mile 105.5
Access road to Quesnel Lake at Sucker Point.

Mile 106
Community of HORSEFLY. Described on a side trip at Mile 120.2. From here it is 23 miles to the Cariboo Highway near 150 Mile House and Williams Lake.

The mileage and descriptions now resume just north of 100 Mile on the Cariboo Highway.

Mile 73.9

Leaving Bonaparte Game Management Area 14 and entering Horse-fly 19.

PUFFBALLS suddenly appear in many fields after a rain and are quite edible. The flesh is sliced thickly and fried in butter. Some of these balls grow to great size — the report of one monster weighing 15 pounds and measuring 4 feet 6 inches is on record.

As well as being eaten, puffballs were also used as a styptic to stop bleeding by barber-surgeons of the Middle Ages and are still used for this purpose by gypsies and some country people in Europe today.

There are actually two species of puffball in B.C. The Giant puffball and the Gemmed puffball are edible when the inside is white and firm. Both are easily recognized.

Mile 76.5

TATTON ROAD to the west leads to Tatton station on the P.G.E. line. The station is named for Tatton Park, Cheshire, England, formerly the home of Lord Egerton, who bought the 105 Mile Ranch in 1912. At about the same time the Marquis of Exeter was buying the Bridge Creek Ranch at the 100 Mile House.

WATSON MANSION   Near Tatton station is the once lovely, stately mansion built in about 1909 by Captain Watson. Designed by a Victoria architect the house was home to Watson for only a few years, for with the coming of World War One he returned to his command and died overseas.

In 1928 the house was occupied by Major Cowan who managed the Highland Ranch, a large holding which extended practically from 100 Mile to Lac la Hache. Since then vandals have torn the interior apart and completely stripped the house of its original grandeur.

Mile 76.7

105 MILE RANCH AND LAKE   105 Mile House was first built in the 1800's, when it was owned and operated by Mrs. Simon Philipeno. Prior to this, much of the land was owned by Paddy Powers. In 1903 the ranch was sold to Ben McNeil, who built the present buildings around 1909, after a fire had destroyed the original house. Then Lord Egerton purchased the property and finally Fred Davis became the owner in 1948. At present it is being developed in conjunction with the housing project at 108 Mile.

Mile 78
108 MILE RECREATION CENTRE. This is a planned recreational community in the heart of the Cariboo country with forty square miles of natural parkland and year-round accommodation. '108' Golf Course is open from April to September.

Mile 80

108 MILE RANCH   The histories of Tatton, 105 Mile and 108 Mile are closely interwoven. It appears that the first substantial buildings were erected by Steve Tingley, the famous express driver, and operated by his son Clarence as a stopping place for the travelling public. In 1900 the ranch was sold to Captain Watson who built the Tatton mansion and a large barn was put up to house his Clydesdales. After Watson was killed the property was bought by

The old 108 Mile Ranch building, now abandoned, first built by Steve Tingley.

Lord Egerton of 105 Mile and then by Fred Davis. Now it too is being developed into a housing project.

SANDHILL CRANES   These large birds are sometimes seen feeding in the fields around 108 Mile and it is thought by some local people that they nest on Chimney Lake. Their shape is very similar to that of the Whooping crane but the Sandhills are grey with a red topknot. Cranes are also similar in size and shape to the large herons, often erroneously referred to as cranes. However, a heron flies with his neck in an S shape while the crane's neck is outstretched.

Mile 83

111 MILE HOUSE   Situated on 111 Mile Creek. Like most of the early stopping places and ranches, this stop saw many owners. In the 1880's it was the property of William Abel, a local school teacher who decided to become a farmer and innkeeper. The stop was used to change horses and the grain Abel grew was sold to the express companies. In about 1900 Captain Watson bought it along with the 108 Mile property. The old buildings and the cabin with the framed end gable probably date back to one of the early owners.

SPRING LAKE ROAD   Leads to the east and Spring and Dempsey Lakes.

PROTECTED FLOWERS   British Columbia has three protected flowers: the dogwood, our provincial flower; the trillium, and the wild rhododendron. You are not likely to see either the dogwood or the rhododendron but you should see the trillium.

This beautiful little flower also goes by two other names, wake-robin and birthroot — the latter because it was used by the Indians during childbirth.

Trillium is one of the first signs of spring and it is usually seen from March to June, as soon as the snow disappears. At the same time male red-winged blackbirds are defending their nesting territories.

The trillium may be recognized by the large single white flower. It has three petals and three leaves and is from 8 to 16 inches tall. Look for it in the shade, in damp woods and boggy areas.

Mile 83.8

112 MILE HOUSE   The house has long since disappeared but nearby are the remains of John King's blacksmith shop and outbuildings.

FENCES Just north of 112 Mile are good examples of two common types of Cariboo fencing. On the east is the Russell, an economical type used where timber is available and the ground too hard for posts. They are often made from old snakerail fences, such as are seen to the west. The snake is very expensive to build, due to the quantity of material but it is one of the strongest. Another advantage is that a panel is easily removed to drive stock through. A snake fence will use some 2500 logs per mile and last forty years.

Mile 86

The old buildings on the west side of the highway have been empty for over fifty years, a reminder of the early settlers and ranchers of the Lac La Hache region. The 114 Mile Ranch was not a stopping place for the general public, although it was used on occasion for public meetings and concerts. It was built in 1891 by Peter Hamilton, the son of Gavin Hamilton, a fur-factor who had married one of Peter Ogden's daughters. The ranch is now part of the Flying 5 holdings.

Mile 86.9

FLYING 5 RANCH, cabins and an antique shop. Once the site of 115 Mile House, built in 1862 by Archibald McKinley.

The Water Ouzel or dipper can be found in many streams.

Mile 87.2

A side road to the east leads to several lakes, including Spout and Timothy. At Mile 4.6 the road forks. Keep left for Spout and right for Timothy. Three miles along the Timothy Lake road is Green Lake with a natural boat launching site.

On the Spout Lake fork the road passes Rail Lake at Mile 13.4 and Spout Lake at Mile 18. A few miles farther is another junction, with the right leading to the Murphy Lakes and straight ahead leading to McIntosh and eventually the settlement of Horsefly. A left fork after the Murphy Lake junction takes you along a road down Knife Creek to 141 Mile House and the Cariboo Highway.

BIRDS There are over 253 species of birds that have been recorded in the Cariboo, many of which nest and breed here. A few of these, however, are quite rare and are only seen once or twice in a decade. One of these is the Bobolink, last seen in this area in 1959. The male is easily identified by his contrasting black and white plumage and buff neck. He is associated with broad open fields of tall grass. His ecstatic banjo-like song is delivered either while perched or while in slow flight with rapid shallow wing strokes. Watch for him and if you see one, report the sighting to Anna Roberts of Williams Lake.

Yellow-bellied Sapsucker — one of many Cariboo birds.

A female yellow-headed blackbird with a bill full of insects for her brood.

Mile 87.3

LAC LA HACHE Elevation 2761. Population 1500. Lake of the Axe is both a small supply community and a 12-mile long lake. The French name probably originated when one of the early settlers tried to chop a hole in the ice for water and lost his axe. The Indians called it "Lake Pretty Waters".

The first store in Lac La Hache was built and run by Isaac Ogden, born at Fort St. James in 1859 and grandson of Peter Skene Ogden, an early employee of the Hudson's Bay Company. The log store was built on a small flat above the highway and although it was hidden from sight of the road most of the early inhabitants knew its location. Isaac was married to a native of the country, Rose Eagle (whose father founded the Onward ranch near Williams Lake) and because of his years of living with Indians at Fort St. James the local Indians found that they could trust him and believe in him. Consequently Ogden served as Indian agent throughout his life.

In 1922 Isaac obtained the mail contract and opened a small post-office in his general store, with himself as postmaster. It has been in the Ogden family ever since, with Hugh Ogden, a grandson of Isaac, holding the position at present.

Mile 88.1

According to one source this little log cabin at 117 Mile was originally pre-empted and filed on, for the fee of $5.00 by Gus Anderson. Later John Gannon came into the crown grant and lived there with his family for many years. He mortgaged the home for $1000 to Oppenheimer Bros. of Vancouver. Then Mrs. Gannon got tired of the place, or mad at John and left, tearing up the grant. John stayed for awhile but did not have the money to legally prove title, so he left, telling Joe Harrington, who had been living with him, that if he could straighten things out he could have the place. Joe didn't, but he lived there for many years until his death. Then other families used the building off and on until it was 'gazetted' in the B.C. Gazette by Oppenheimers. Finally in about 1935 G. W. Felker bought it and made the cabin part of the Flying 5 Ranch.

Mile 93

KOKANEE LODGE Greyhound bus stop and public access to Lac La Hache.

This lodge, built in 1952, replaced the original, ivy-covered 122 Mile House, one of the earliest stopping places on the Cariboo road. In 1867 it was being operated by the Walter brothers and was known as an excellent place to lodge or have a meal. George Forbes and his wife bought the property from Thomas McDougall in 1893 after arriving from Aberdeen, Scotland. Most of the adjoining ranch lands and meadows still belong to the Forbes family ranch, located a short distance north.

GENEOLOGY Tracing families and the ownership of lands in the Cariboo can result in a great deal of confusion. Because of the small populations in the early days, and the large families, there was considerable intermarriage among the early settlers. Also, many of the early fur-traders and factors married Indian women, who gave them large families of sons and daughters. Consequently the confusion of Christian and family names makes research very difficult. Many sons were named after their father. Another source of confusion was the fact that death often removed a parent at an early age and a second or third or fourth marriage followed. For instance in the Lac La Hache area the Ogdens, Hamiltons, McKinleys, Eagles and McDougalls were all related by marriage. In many cases the descendants, now married into still more families with greatly increased numbers, live in the same region, controlling large historic ranches or operating various services.

Mile 96

LAC LA HACHE PARK This wooded campsite contains 29 picnic tables and 84 campsites. Drinking water is available and swimming is safe, although parents should watch children and guard them from the danger of high speed traffic on the highway.

LOONS The night air is still. Only the lap of water on the lakeshore can be heard, or perhaps the soft sigh of a breeze running through the leaves of an aspen on its way to the lake. A call breaks the silence — a long mournful call, almost human at time, rippling across the water and through the chill night air. It is the call of the loon, a sound synonymous with wildness and the North.

The common loon is seen on most of the larger lakes of the Cariboo, though usually only one family to a lake. They are a large water bird, living on fish and swimming low in the water. The head and neck are a glossy black with a broken white collar or necklace. The back is checkered with black and white.

It is said that loons can forecast the coming of a storm. Before spells of heavy rain or wind they become wildly excited and during gales they rise from the lake and fly head into the wind, as if gaining a sense of power in the strength of their flight and the rush of the wind over their feathers.

The Déné Indians have a beautiful story about the loon. It illustrates how the native people revered the animals and the elements and how they considered themselves as part of nature's plan, not the supreme beings at the top of the ladder as modern man does.

Once there was an old man who was blind. Although he was blind, he had great magic in his spittle. His wife helped him hunt and in this way he managed to live. Each time his wife sighted game, she handed him one of his arrows which he moistened with his spittle. Then his wife would point his bow towards the game and when he let his arrow go it never missed its mark.

One day they came upon a very fat caribou. His wife handed him an arrow saying, "Quick, wet the arrow head with your spittle." After he had done this and released his arrow, the caribou fell dead. But his wife wanted the caribou for herself and she was tired of looking after a blind man, so she pretended he had missed and pushed him to the ground saying, "That old good-for-nothing! What a bad shot he is!" Then the old man was very sad. He could not find the caribou. As he looked for it he wandered far away, so his wife cut up the meat and what she did not eat she hung up to dry.

After a long time the old man came to a lake and sat there making loud cries of sadness. A loon came to him and asked why he cried so. "Alas," said the man, "I am blind and my wife has left me." Then the loon said, "Come to me and sit on my back and bury your eyes in the down of my neck." The man did so and they both plunged beneath the water. When they came to the surface, the loon asked, "Can you see now?" And the old man replied, "I see a little as though through a mist." Then the loon dived again and this time he rose to the surface, the old man could see very well. He was grateful to the loon, but the only thing he had to give to him was his most prized possession — his necklace of dentalium shells. This he threw towards the loon and it settled around the bird's neck. Then he took a few other shells from the bottom of his quiver and threw them and they settled on the loon's back. And that is how the loon got his necklace and his marks!

Mile 97

WRIGHT STATION, at the end of Lac La Hache, is the P.G.E. station for 127 Mile Ranch, originally established by William Wright to supply the miners of the Cariboo goldfields with meat and dairy produce. William Wright and his son John came to the Cariboo with the Overlanders in 1862. They chose a location near 137 Mile but later traded with Mike McCarthy for the 127 Mile Ranch. After more than 100 years the 127 is still operated by the family.

82

WILD ROSE In B.C. there are at least 6 different species of wild rose, each having a fragrant perfume and white to deep rose flowers. The leaves have an odd number of leaflets and a wing-like sheaf clasps the base of the leaf. The fruit, also called 'hips', hangs on all winter and can be used as a source of Vitamin C. Here is an Indian recipe you might like to try, particularly if you have a cold or rheumatism:

Collect a quantity of rose hips. Remove trimmings, barely cover with water and boil until soft (about 15 minutes). Put the resulting mixture through a sieve. Add one cup of sugar to two cups of the puree and boil down to half quantity.

One teaspoon of this is equal in Vitamin C content to one orange and may be stored for one year. Take one teaspoonful a day, or more if you have a cold or rheumatism.

Whistling Swan — often seen during spring migrations.

Mile 99

127 MILE HOUSE In the 1860's a stopping place was being established here and during construction business was transacted in a large blue tent, owned by George Felker. From that time on it was the 'Blue Tent Ranch'. In May 1863 a miner walking to Richfield wrote, "Travelled 28 miles, feel a little tired. My feet quite sound. Some of our party in a bad state with sore feet. Put up at the 'Blue Tent'. Paid $1.50 for supper and slept comfortably on the floor."

SNAKES Most of B.C.'s snakes are found south of the Cache Creek - Kamloops area. One in particular ranges north of this. In fact it is found as far north as Aiyansh and east to the Peace River District. This is the Northwestern or Striped Garter snake. His color is dark brown or black above, usually with three greenish-yellow, yellow, bluish, or greyish stripes running from the back of the head to the tip of the tail. Between the middle and lateral stripes a series of red blotches are produced by a red coloration of the skin between the scales. This reptile will often take to the water when disturbed and because of this is sometimes called a 'water snake'.

Another snake, the Wandering Garter Snake, is also found north of this line. It has a pronounced spotted appearance and is also fond of water. It is the most aggressive of all the garter snakes and will strike fiercely and accurately when cornered, sometimes inflicting a painful wound with its sharp teeth. It is not venomous.

Mile 101

130 MILE LAKE AND RANCH, owned by the Wright Cattle Company. In early spring, just as the ice is beginning to melt, it is quite common to see one or more bald eagles sitting on the edge of the ice in this lake. More may be soaring overhead or perched in the tall trees along the shore. These birds are migrating north to their nesting grounds. Eagles' numbers have dropped drastically since the Second World War due to the increased use of hard-core pesticides.

Mile 102.3

132 MILE HOUSE, an early ranch originally owned by the Ulrichs. Many of the Houses in the Lac La Hache area were not actually stopping places but were named by the mileage method to avoid confusion and make identification easy.

Mile 104.5   Stop of Interest

TO THE GOLDFIELDS In the 1860's the fabulous Cariboo goldfields were a lure to thousands. Miners, traders and adventurers, many

afoot, some, with wheelbarrows, shared the pioneer route with mule trains, plodding oxen, freight wagons and swaying stagecoaches. Havens for man and beast were the Road Houses and stables every twelve to fourteen miles along the way.

Mile 105

134 MILE RANCH   In 1910 this stage stop for the Tingley mail carrier was being managed by John Ross for Dave Stoddart.

Mile 107.3

The site of McCarthy's 137 MILE HOUSE. The old buildings seen here have a dovetail corner. This unique feature made it almost impossible for corners to pull apart. The compound angles cut into the logs stop movement in any direction.

First owned by the Wrights, 137 Mile Ranch was traded to Mike McCarthy.

Dovetail corners give many old buildings a stability lacking in most log construction.

LICHENS (Pronounced, 'That's a lie, Ken!') Lichens are small flowerless plants which can flourish on bare rock. They are composed of greenish or bluish algae cells which are preyed on by fungi cells, the combined organisms being called lichens.

It can be quite interesting to see how many types you can identify. They make excellent subjects for micro-photography. Lichens can also be used as a source of dye. The pigment can be extracted by either soaking the plant in an ammonia solution or boiling in water. A little experimenting will show you which species will produce what color, but color can be deepened or altered by addition of a little acid. For instance it will deepen the yellow of Letharia.

Almost anything in the wild can be eaten and lichens are no exception. A particularly good recipe has been recorded for those who are game for anything. Take a handful of old-man's-beard lichen, the small green plant often seen in trees and boil it with a medium size rock, vigorously, for about 20-25 minutes. For the best taste, when the lichen appears done, throw it away and eat the rock.

Mile 109.3

The small community of 140 MILE. Unincorporated. Hinsche road to the east joins Knife Creek road.

Mile 110.5

Knife Creek road, a good gravel road, leads east. It follows Knife Creek past Squawk Lake and joins the Lac La Hache to Horsefly road just north of the Murphy Lake junction.

Mile 111

The ranch on your right was 141 MILE HOUSE, situated on Knife Creek and settled in 1862 by the Murphys.

SPEEDOMETER TEST SECTION mile zero is at this point.

WOODCHUCKS AND MARMOTS Whenever we see these interesting rodents at the side of the road or running across a field, we are reminded of the childhood tongue twister which went, "How much wood would a woodchuck chuck if a woodchuck would chuck wood?"

Three species reside in B.C. and there is a good chance of your seeing all of them on your travels up the Cariboo Road. From Cache Creek to Williams Lake you will see the yellow-bellied marmot. In fact, a particularly good den is located near Mile 112. The sides of the marmot's neck are yellow; this, with the white nose and shorter front claws, distinguishes him from the wood-chuck, who is darker and found farther north.

The hoary marmot or whistler is found in the alpine regions in most of B.C. and can weigh as much as 30 pounds. His human-like whistle is most distinctive and he is usually lighter in color than either of the other two species.

OSPREY   It is quite likely that while driving through the Cariboo country in the spring or summer you will see overhead, or diving into a lake, a large brown and white bird only slightly smaller than the bald eagle. This is the osprey, sometimes referred to as the 'fish hawk'.
The osprey nests much like the eagle, in the very tops of trees or snags, building a hugh eyrie of branches or twigs. One such nest is located to the west of the town of Williams Lake, on the hill overlooking the Dog Creek road. The birds are often seen near the town as they travel to and from feeding areas. Another nest is near Chimney Lake, west of Williams Lake off the Dog Creek road. Osprey are also reported to nest on Crooked Lake, near Quesnel Lake.

These beautiful birds of prey are rapidly declining in number due to man's use of pesticides, as are all of the fish-eating birds. Like the eagle and the white pelican in this region their eggs are much weaker and frequently break while the parent bird incubates.

The osprey catches his food by diving into a lake or river, seizing a fish in his talons and surfacing. After emerging the fish is turned lengthways in the osprey's talons so that there is less wind resist-ance. Osprey can be distinguished from other large hawks by his 'crooked' wings, which show black at the carpal or wrist joints. They will also hover over the water before diving. They breed over most of North America, lay two to four eggs and have a wingspan of 4½ to 6 feet.

Mile 115.4

MISSION ROAD or San Jose Valley road. This good gravel road leads past the St. Joseph Mission and the Cariboo Indian School to the railway station of Onward and the Onward Ranch, now part of the Mission. The road runs past the Sugar Cane Reserve and rejoins the highway at Mile 120.5.

FOLK SONGS   There are very few folk songs written in or about B.C., probably due to the fact that our history is relatively young and many of the songs sung were not new songs but rather those brought over from other countries. One, however, that is native to our province is 'Klondike'—song written after the original Cariboo goldrush, when people were using this road and others to reach areas farther afield.

> Oh! come with me where the treasure lies hid
> Come with me where there's gold,
> Where a hatful of mud is a five-pound note,
> And a clod on your head is a quid!

Chorus: Klondike, Klondike,
> Label your luggage for Klondike,
> For there ain't no luck in this town today,
> Ain't no work down Moodyville way,
> So pack up your bags and be off I say,
> Off and away to the Klondike.

> Oh, they scratches the earth and it tumbles out,
> More than your hands can hold,
> For the hills above and the plains beneath,
> Are cracking and busting with gold.

Mile 118

PIGEON ROAD, a twelve-mile gravel road to the east following Borland Creek to its headquarters. Named for the Pigeon family who established a ranch at Meadow Lake in the Chilcotin.

Mile 118.4

150 MILE HOUSE was an important junction during the wagon days for this was the point where freight and passengers transferred to stages heading to the Chilcotin country or east to the goldfields near Likely and Keithley Creek. The Cariboo Road was to have passed west of 150 Mile, closer to the shores of Williams Lake. However, the contractors, Wright and Galbraith, needed a loan to complete the construction and were turned down by Tom Manifee of Williams Lake. The Davidson Bros., who had started farming here in 1861, offered to lend the money on the condition that the road be routed past 150 Mile. Since the contractors were able to locate the road where they wished, this was quickly done and now travellers branch off to reach Williams Lake.

The Davidsons sold 150 Mile and in 1876 a man named Bates sold it to Gavin Hamilton, chief factor with the H.B.C. at Fort St. James. Hamilton's son later established 114 Mile Ranch at Mile 87, near Lac La Hache. In 1886 Gavin sold the place to Veith and Borland who built the business up and sold after 15 years to an English company for a reported $90,000.

Mile 118.6

Junction. The road to Horsefly and Quesnel turns right and the road to Williams Lake and the new main road fork left. The road to Keithley Creek is a side trip.

This junction leads to a whole new area for the traveller to explore. It was the original route to the goldfields. The main road joins up with the new highway near Soda Creek and is the original route of the Cariboo road. Until recently the Williams Lake route was a business route to the town, with most of the traffic following this road.

Mile 2.7

A junction to the right leading 21 miles to Horsefly. As you can probably guess its name comes from the rather large 'carnivourous' flies associated with this country. This was where gold was first discovered in 1859 by Peter Dunlevy, an American who with his companions was probably the first white man to see the Horsefly River. Nearby Horsefly Lake is 35 miles long and 2 miles wide, with fishing for rainbow and lake trout. This route is described further at Mile 72.5 on Highway 97.

DUNLEVY Peter Curran Dunlevy, born in Pittsburgh, Pa., U.S.A. on October 21, 1834, was the first white man to discover gold in the Cariboo. In May of 1859 Dunlevy and his companions Jim Sellers, Tom Manifee, Tom Moffitt and Ira Crow, were camped at the mouth of the Chilcotin River, where they were prospecting for gold. They happened to meet and befriend an Indian scout of the Shuswap tribe, Tomaah, who in return for their hospitality offered to show them where gold the size of beans could be found. Journeying down to Lillooet and then across to Fort Kamloops they purchased more horses and equipment and then proceeded north to Lac La Hache where they had arranged to meet Tomaah. This was a meeting place for various Indian tribes where yearly games were held and trading accomplished.

Here they were introduced to Baptiste, a tall, strong Indian who later became a guide and companion for Judge Matthew Begbie. Some days later, on about June 16, Baptiste led the miners to Horsefly River and the coarse gold they were searching for. It is estimated that the Dunlevy party took out over 1 million dollars in gold.

Dunlevy later opened a stopping place at Beaver Lake and then in 1863, leaving Jim Sellers in charge of the spread, he opened the Colonial Hotel at Soda Creek. He married a Déné girl from Alexandria who left when he married Jane Huston of Victoria, by whom he had a daughter Canissa. In 1882 he had another daughter, Gertrude, by his third wife, Jennie Holstein.

In 1881 Isabella Dunlevy, presumably a daughter from his Déné wife, married Samuel Withrow who, with Tom Hance and Riske, started the first ranches in the Chilcotin country.

On October 15, 1904 Peter Dunlevy, the founder of the Cariboo gold rush, died and was buried in the churchyard at St. Joseph's Mission. (Mile 115.4.)

Mile 3
Site of Crosina's 153 Mile House.

Mile 7

158 MILE HOUSE, MOUNTAIN HOUSE   After crossing over Carpenter's Mountain we come to the former site of 158 Mile, situated on the south fork of Hawks Creek, at the junction of the Cariboo Wagon Road and the Gold Fields Trail. About six miles down the left fork, the Cariboo road, you will come to the Deep Creek Indian Reserve and Deep Creek. Frank Way's 164 Mile House was in this area but it was closed sometime prior to 1899, so it is doubtful if anything remains. Our mileage now follows the Gold Fields Trail, east to Keithley Creek.

Mile 15.6

BIG LAKE   A popular area for guest ranches and a good lake for rainbow trout. Ruffed grouse and moose are abundant in this area.

Mile 23
A good road to the northwest, or left, 26 miles to the highway 97 at McLeese Lake.

Mile 23.5
BEAVER CREEK AND BRIDGE   A side road right leads to Horsefly Lake and left to some small lakes. A small store-cafe is here. Originally there were two stores, a gambling house and an animal market. The store was owned by a Frenchman, François Guy and it was for years called Guy's Place. The buildings vanished and the land passed to the Hamilton family, descendants of Gavin Hamilton, the fur-factor.

Mile 35.6
MOREHEAD LAKE   We cross the creek over Morehead Dam, holding back the waters of Morehead Lake, a man-made reservoir to provide a head for the hydraulic pumps at Bullion.

Secretive and shy, the cougar is seldom seen.

Mile 38.5
HYDRAULIC, a small settlement.

Mile 41.5
A side road to the left to the ghost town of BULLION. This road, crossing Dancing Bill's Gulch, was also the road to Quesnel Forks before the bridge across the river was washed away in the spring floods.

Bullion. A gold strike originally made by Dancing Bill, Thomas Latham, in 1859. He took out as high as $110 per day, and when it appeared to peter out he moved on. But the wily Chinese moved in and twenty years later they were working an old river channel they had found 125 feet above the river and 1000 feet back. They reportedly took out some $900,000. Then in 1892 J. B. Hobson came up with an idea for hydraulic mining. The following year the Cariboo Hydraulic Mining Co. was formed and in 1897 it was reorganized as the Consolidated Hydraulic Mining Co. Ltd. Hobson was mine manager and his first project in mining the 10-mile area was to make a ditch or canal 21 miles long, to collect the water from Boot Jack Lake and Pelley Lake for his hydraulic pumps. In six years, $1,250,000 was taken out.

In 1898 Hobson constructed the dam and Morehead reservoir which you passed a few miles back, at a cost of $118,000. But hydraulicing required a great deal of water and there was a shortage of sources. The constant, costly searching forced the company to look for more financing. This was found but the new financiers eventually closed the mine down and until 1932 it was worked very little.

In 1932 the mine was reopened and during the next ten years more gold was brought out than had been thought possible. Eventually the gold was finished and the town of Bullion was abandoned.

The large house still standing was Hobson's and if you look hard you will see the remains of a few more. Soon they will all have passed into memory. But the yawning depths of the Bullion Pit will remain, a marker to man's never ceasing search for wealth.

Mile 45.9

A bridge over the Quesnel River and the community of Likely. Here the river is navigable to its source in Quesnel Lake, approximately three miles upstream. The strong current makes a strong engine mandatory, however. Situated in a valley ringed by 7,000-foot peaks, at an elevation of 2380 feet above sea level, Quesnel Lake is B.C.'s ninth largest.

Mile 46

LIKELY Russian potatoes? It seems that when the early Russian fur-traders were on the B.C. coast some 200 years ago, they brought with them some strangely shaped Siberian potatoes. Somehow these potatoes got to the site of Cedar City, on the shores of Quesnel Lake, where Captain Evans-Atkinson, a placer miner of Likely, came across them. Here is his story, as told in the B.C. Wildlife Review.

"When I arrived in Cedar Creek on snowshoes during the goldrush more than 40 years ago I was served a meal of beaver tails and Russian potatoes. I inquired and found that the spuds were growing wild on the site of Cedar City. I dug some up and have been growing them ever since

"I suppose the potatoes were brought in from the coast by the early traders who had contact with the Russians who were then on the coast. Some potatoes were discarded and took root.

"A few placer miners still use them because they are so easy to cook. You don't peel them, you just boil them and eat them. They are quite tasty and are a real link with the past."

Mile 46.3

QUESNEL FORKS, a few miles down this side road, lies at the junction of the Cariboo and Quesnel River and is without a doubt one of the finest ghost towns in B.C.

It lies on the original gold fields trail to Barkerville and was a stopping place for all the men who made the region famous: Billy Barker, William Deitz, Doc Keithly and many more.

The townsite was surveyed by the Royal Engineers in 1861 as a supply center for the many small camps and towns in the gold fields. Most of the main buildings were extremely well made, with dovetailed corners and good rafters. When we last visited the town the Chinese Masonic Temple or Joss House was still standing and the beams still had Chinese characters written on them. The town is now inhabited by a couple of prospectors who look for lost claims in the hills, or gold in the creeks. Quesnel Forks is a fine example of an early gold town and should be preserved, or at least protected from the ravages of the unrelenting river erosion.

Quesnel Forks in 1899. This exceptionally sharp photo was taken by J. H. Blome, a professional photographer located at Grand Forks, Clinton and Ashcroft. Vancouver City Archives photo.

LOG DRIVES   A couple of years ago the Cariboo and Quesnel Rivers were the site of a conflict between conservationists and some of the local logging companies. The Weldwood company was using the rivers as a convenient, economical method of transport to the mill site, saving some miles of hauling by truck. The logs could be dumped in at various spots in Cariboo Lake or along the rivers and then pulled out at the mill near Quesnel. But many others took a different view. They felt that the river, its banks and its life were being damaged by the drives — mainly because of inadequate protection by stringers and buffer logs. In numerous places erosion was being hastened by the buffeting of logs; in fact, a prospector lost a cabin to erosion. After a public outcry additional protection was given to the troublesome spots, but the public, the conservationists and Rod and Gun Club members want *no* log driving. Whether this is to be remains to be seen. If they are still being driven when you are reading this section they can be seen either at the Forks or at various side roads leading north to the Quesnel river between Likely and Morehead Lake, or at the town of Quesnel itself.

Mile 47

 Another fork in the road. The right leads to the lake and the former site of Cedar City. A public government campsite and boat launching site are located at Cedar Point Park. At press time there were no facilities and only rough campsites.

The roads in this area are constantly changing due to logging but at last report there was a good logging access road from Likely to Keithley Creek, crossing the Cariboo River between the two towns.

Keithley Creek never amounted to much in the way of permanent buildings but during the rush it was home to 10,000 miners. This was 1860 and the peak of the rush to the wealth of the Cariboo, with most of the miners living in tents.

From here to Barkerville is 25 miles, quite a spectacular trip when the road is passable. However, like Bruce Ramsey, we were turned back by a washed out bridge. As well as passing many old claims and the ghost town of Antler Creek, you will climb to an elevation of 6200 feet in the Yanks Peak region. This beautiful area has been constantly suggested as an alpine park but at the time of writing it is still used for the grazing of domestic sheep.

From Yanks Peak the road follows Cunningham Creek and then goes through Cunningham Pass. Stevens Gulch and then Beggs Gulch are on the left and then Antler Creek on the right. The old town of Grouse Creek is somewhere to the left after this, marked by a couple of tumbled down cabins. Then we cross Williams Creek and arrive in Barkerville.

If you have travelled this route from Cache Creek you have followed in the footsteps of countless thousands of would-be miners and fortune seekers who trekked from all over the world to search for and discover the gold of Williams Creek, and who walked in before the Cariboo Road was begun.

Our mileage and descriptions now resume just north of 150 Mile House on the main Cariboo Road, Highway 97.

Mile 120.5
Mission Road leads left to the Sugar Cane Indian village, little changed in 100 years.

Mile 123
You are now passing WILLIAM'S LAKE, so called on the Geographical Journal map of 1861 and named after either Jack Williams, a Cornish settler, or Chief William, a chief of the Sugar Cane Indians. Elevation of the lake is 1859 feet.

Sugar Cane Indian Reserve with Williams Lake in the background. Although this · photo was taken in 1899, the village is little changed. Vancouver City Archives photo.

A campsite, operated by the city of Williams Lake, is located on Scout Island at the west end of the lake. Watch for signs as you near the town.

WESTERN GREBES Breed in decreasing numbers on the lake. This large, graceful grebe, with its long, very slender neck and sharply contrasted black and white coloration, is being driven from more and more lakes by the roar of outboard engines. Its breeding display is one of the most spectacular in the bird world, especially when two birds rear up vertically and race side by side over the water surface.

A good hay crop on the Buckhorn Ranch, Chilcotin, B.C.

Mile 126.5

 The high bluff on the right hand side of the road, across from the Bil-Nor Restaurant is known as SENTINEL ROCK or SIGNAL POINT. Judge Henry Castillou, a noted authority on Indian lore, says that this was the meeting place of an ancient tribe of Indians of the Athapaskan language group. They called the lake Clumneetza or Columneetza and it is thought this word could be the same as cum to neetza or, translated, the meeting place of princely people.

However this may be, it is probable that the bluff is an old signal point where a warrior could stand and signal up or down the lake, across to the Dog Creek Road or as far as the Sugar Cane Reserve.

Mile 127

 On your left you can now see the Stampede grounds and the road

Indian woman and an old wagon wheel in the Cariboo country.   Keith C. Smith photo.

Stagecoach driver at Barkerville.

to Scout Island Campground which is also a bypass to the Dog Creek and Chilcotin roads.

The mountain to your right was, until 1960, the site of the exciting Mountain Horse Race, begun in 1921. Starting on the ridge high above the grounds the riders raced their horses down the steep hill, jumped across the then gravel Cariboo road, rode down the remaining slope and one quarter of the way around the track. The race was cancelled in 1960 because of the increased traffic on the paved highway and the number of houses on the trail route.

Mile 127.5

Junction. Left to the town of Williams Lake and the Chilcotin country and right to Quesnel.

WILLIAMS LAKE Originally the land belonged to the Sugar Cane Indians who granted substantial holdings to William Pinchback. He later sold the land to Borland and Comer who established large ranches. Upper house was on the Comer Ranch, located above Glendale, while Lower Borland House, built by Pinchback, was in the area of the present Stampede grounds. Pinchback also built a flour mill on Williams Lake Creek in 1884. The creek was the site of Borland Post Office.

In 1919, on fields still growing grain, a new town was being surveyed. The P.G.E. railway was coming through and crops were the least of the worries of the district. Everyone was trying to get his business built and in operation first. Cattle and horses were soon replaced with buildings and in 1920 Borland became the town of Williams Lake.

A few years later, in 1925, Reverend A. D. MacKinnon visited the town and described it as follows:

"When I began in 1921 there were no homes, the people living in tents and camps on the townsite. There are many fine houses at present and the place is growing steadily. There are two schools, four hotels, four stores, two halls, a Masonic hall, a moving picture house, a hospital and the best Provincial Building in the Interior."

Today Williams Lake is a regional administration center for the courts, Land Office, Fish and Wildlife Branch, R.C.M.Police and Forestry. It is the major supply center for the Cariboo and Chilcotin ranchers and tourist camps. Visitors will find all the usual tourist needs and a good selection of motels.

POINTS OF INTEREST around Williams Lake include a number of interesting day trips by road. For instance, the old road to Soda Creek, north on the Fraser, could be followed to Soda Creek and then back on the main highway, or you could turn west at Rudy Johnson's private bridge, just south of Soda Creek.

This bridge, probably the only privately owned toll bridge in B.C., was built by rancher Rudy Johnson. The structure was bought from the Alaska Highways Department for $40,000 and transported to this location for $160,000. (Of course, engineers said it couldn't be done.) Logging trucks pay toll according to weight and distance saved. Private vehicles are free. The government bridge is at the Sheep Creek crossing, 17 miles south. As well as saving the loggers many miles Rudy also saves 39 miles from his Buckskin Ranch to Williams Lake.

Following this road across the bridge will take you to the Meldrum Creek road, where you can turn north to Quesnel or south to the Bella Coola road just west of Sheep Creek hill. It makes a good circle trip to Williams Lake.

Another trip would be the 300-mile journey across the vast Chilcotin plateau to Bella Coola. Here you pass names like Riske Creek, Alexis Creek, Anahim and Atnarko, the land of Ralph Edwards and Rich Hobson. But this is another story, another book. Here is B.C.'s last cattle frontier.

Mile 134
Turnoff to the Williams Lake airport.

INDIANS   The journal of Simon Fraser, Friday June 3rd, 1808.

"This is called the Atnah Nation. Their country is well stocked with large animals and they consequently pay very little attention to fishing. In summer they reside in shades, and their winter quarters which are built under ground are square below diminishing gradually in size to the top, where there is a small aperture which serves the double purpose of door and chimney, while a post with notches answers for a pair of stairs."

This would be the Déné language group, as somewhere in this area the Salish changed to Déné.

Mile 141.6
DEEP CREEK PICNIC SITE   Have you ever wondered why at a developed picnic site the tables are in a particular spot? Well, studies have shown that picnickers seldom use a table that is more than 250 feet from their car. Very little use was made of tables 300 feet away and at 400 feet they were not used at all.

Mile 141.8
Side road to the right or southeast. This is the original Cariboo

Brunson Lake on the Chimney Lake Road near Williams Lake.

Quesnel Forks, surveyed by the Royal Engineers in 1861, has only a few buildings still standing.

100

The Fraser River in the Chilcotin area.

road route. It leads to Likely and Horsefly junctions before it again meets the main highway at 150 Mile House. It is described at Mile 120.2.

ROAD HOUSES 164 Mile House and later 158 Mile House, which lie up the last side road, were the last Houses on the road. From Soda Creek a sternwheeler was usually taken and if a traveller needed a room the local ranches served the purpose. The Road Houses were an important part of the Cariboo's history and the pleasure of our travels will be less without them.

Mile 148.5

Road to SODA CREEK; the end of the Cariboo road from 1863 to 1865 and the departure point for sternwheelers heading up the Fraser from 1863 to 1921. This route was eventually served by nine ships with the *Enterprise* being the first. She was built in 1863 by contractor G. B. Wright at a cost of $75,000, the machinery and boiler having been packed up the road by mules. Soda Creek soon became a shipyard and the *Enterprise* was followed by the *Chilcotin, B.C. Express, Fort Fraser, Charlotte, Quesnel* and others.

Soda Creek, showing the S.S. Enterprise in foreground. In the background is the Colonial Hotel and Dunlevy's store.

Ships serving the river would stop wherever a white flag was displayed, whether a regular stop or not. In 1924 the steamship *Circle W* was still making occasional trips on the river from Soda Creek to Prince George but the era really ended in 1921 with the wrecking of the *Quesnel* in Fort George Canyon.

Nearby is the grave of Capt. Frank Odin of the steamship *Charlotte.* He was born at Point Roberts, Washington in 1863 and died here at Soda Creek in 1899.

Soda Creek has changed in the last decades and few of the old original buildings are still standing. A couple of them are occupied. Main Street is quiet now with only a few barking dogs to greet the visitor, rather than the hundreds of goldseekers, merchants and rivermen who once made their way along the road.

The town took its name from a creek near here that bubbles like soda water after passing through a formation of carbonate of lime. It has been suggested that nearby there should be a Whiskey Creek.

In 1866 John Adams built a flour mill here, which unfortunately did not pay. Not to be deterred, Adams hauled the boiler and engine to Savona, where he built a stern-wheeler in 1868. The ship ran for several years between Savona and Enderby.

The Soda Creek road, which also leads south to Williams Lake, continues north for 2 miles to the Soda Creek ferry, a reaction ferry crossing to the west bank of the Fraser. Its operating times are 7 to 12 a.m., 1 to 5 p.m. and 6 to 7 p.m. From the ferry the road con-

The Soda Creek Reaction Ferry, like other similar ferries, carries cars to the west bank of the Fraser River.

Watson mansion, abandoned for many years, lies to the west of 105 Mile Ranch.

tinues through farms and ranches. This is once again the original route of the Cariboo road and here the various ranches served as roadhouses. It is a quiet route away from the rush of the main highway, where a curious traveller may easily stop and explore or photograph the ranches and hills. The road reaches Highway 97 at MacAlister, Mile 160.5.

Mile 154.4
McLEESE LAKE, named for a pioneer resident.

BEAVER   One of the main reasons for the exploration of the West, if not *the* reason, is still to be seen in the many lakes of the Cariboo. They are sometimes confused with the more numerous muskrat, but the beaver is larger, has a broad tail rather than a rat-like tail and builds his lodge of branches, unlike the muskrat which uses reeds. The beaver also builds a dam to provide himself with sufficient water for swimming and a place to store winter food.

Mile 154.7

Road to Tyee Lake, 14 miles. A fork a few miles down the road will take you into the Big Lake area and the road to Likely. Tyee is Chinook jargon for 'chief'. This lake was a favorite of Chief William of the Soda Creek band.

Mile 159.6   Stop of Interest Sign

Down-river lay the perilous and unnavigable canyon. Up-river the Fraser was swift and strong, but sternwheelers could travel for 400 miles from Soda Creek. Men and supplies embarked here in the 1860's for the fabulous Cariboo gold fields. Later, as the G.T.P. Railway was forged across the Province, nine paddlewheelers formed a life-line to the North.

Mile 160.5

MacALISTER, a P.G.E. station named after James M. MacAlister, a former postmaster here. The old road via Soda Creek to Williams Lake joins the highway here on the left.

Mile 164.3

The small supply community of MARGUERITE is named after an Indian woman of the Déné group who is said to have drowned more than one of her babies in nearby Marguerite Lake.

Mile 165.2

A cable reaction ferry crosses the Fraser to ranches, farms and saw-mills on the west side. These rather unique ferries are gradually disappearing as more bridges and better roads take their place. An interesting side trip can be taken by crossing here and rejoining the highway at Quesnel.

Mile 166.5

THE McINNES HOUSE   Bruce Ramsey in his book, 'Ghost Towns of B.C.', gives a fairly complete history of this old home and Fort Alexandria. He relates that A. D. McInnes bought the Hudson's Bay Company farmlands in 1860 and that this building was not built by him as it was already in existence when the first miners came up the trails in 1859. It is assumed that the building was part of the Fort, or its out buildings and that the cairn, a couple of miles north, is not in the correct location.

If this was part of the Fort's farm buildings then there is a building down on the Indian reserve which local tradition says is part of the actual fort. It is one mile north and a half mile west next to the old church.

In order to reduce dependency on Fort Colville, south in what became the U.S.A., Peter Skene Ogden had a flour mill built at Fort Alexandria. The grinding stones were made in the U.S. and brought up the old brigade trail through the Okanagan to Kamloops and then to the Fort on horseback. The driving gear for the 24-inch stones was built by a Canadian voyageur in 1842. In 1843 the Fort recorded using some 6,500 bushels of grain.

A townsite of Fort Alexandria was surveyed in the 1860's by the Royal Engineers but nothing ever came of it.

Mile 167.3

THE DEVIL'S PALISADES is the name given locally to a formation on the east side of the highway at this point. The basaltic columns forming the palisades are similar in structure to those in Keremeos Columns Provincial Park and the Giants' Causeway in Ireland. Watch closely as they are partially hidden behind a fringe of trees.

Mile 167.6

A cairn marking the supposed site of Fort Alexandria, named for Alexander Mackenzie. Due to its location high above the river it is doubtful if this is the actual site. The inscription on the cairn reads as follows:

"The last post established by the North West Company west of the Rocky Mountains and marking Sir Alexander Mackenzie's far-thest point in the descent of the Fraser River in 1793. Built in 1821. After 1826, when the trade of New Caledonia found outlet to the Pacific, instead of the Atlantic, it was the point of transfer from the

Ashcroft area. The green fields in the distance are Ashcroft Manor and Cornwall Flats. Oregon Jack hills are on the right in this view from the Hat Creek Road.

land to the water brigade and so it remained until the gold discoveries transformed the conditions."

Mile 168.5
An historic ranch where W. J. Anders once ran a general store.

SCHMOOS   A native of the Cariboo. Not the cartoon variety but rather the type known to rockhounds. The actual schmoo is a sedimentary concretion with an appearance more like that of a schmoo, or a ball, or a sculpture from the art gallery, or a bird or an animal. One thing for sure, they are old—possibly 70 to 130 million years old, dating back to the Paleocene and Cretaceous eras. At that time our concretions started forming around a core such as a pebble or a bit of ground litter. Sometimes one or two concretions were formed within a short distance of each other and eventually they joined, giving a new design to the schmoo. Their beginnings are still a bit of a puzzle to scientists but they are always built up by minerals forming in even concentric formations around a core. It is this pattern which defines it as a schmoo and not a common place mud ball. They can be found in many of the Cariboo rivers and streams and are interesting mementos of a morning's search along a river bed.

Mile 174.3

A pioneer ranch built in the typical fashion of the day with the house on one side of the road and the barn on the other. This was once a stopping place on the old road.

WOOD TICKS These insects have been the source of many rumours and stories as to how dangerous they are and how fast they can kill a person. In truth they can cause death if they bite and are left unattended. This takes several days and death follows only after a period of incapability, when presumably the patient would be taken to a doctor. If the tick is removed, recovery begins almost immediately. The bite is not felt due to a local 'anesthetic' which the tick uses before it begins to suck blood. The best solution is to check yourself thoroughly after hiking in the woods in the spring and summer. If a tick is found, remove him. They generally present little problem but various methods are used. One is to put a hot needle on the tick's backside, or a daub of turpentine on the exposed portion. Check to be sure the head, which is often beneath the victim's skin, is also removed and not left to infect the small wound.

110

The "Devil's Palisades", a basaltic rock formation similar to the Giants Causeway in Ireland.

Sunsets on Cariboo lakes.

112

Mile 178.6

AUSTRALIAN RANCH   In 1863 the three Downes brothers and Andrew Olsen loaded all their possessions on a homemade wheelbarrow and headed north in search of gold. Like many others they homesteaded instead, built a cabin at this spot and cleared and cultivated the land while living on turnips and rabbits. Their first crops were wheat and potatoes, but as they grew more and more produce they began travelling to the mining camps with a two-wheel cart, selling fresh vegetables to the scurvey ridden miners.

The Downes brothers left after a short time but Olsen continued, later selling out to J. M. and Y. Yorston, two stage drivers for the B. X. Co., who developed the ranch further.

Mile 185.6

KERSLEY, named after a pioneer settler, Charles Kersley, who pre-empted land here in 1867.

ROCK HOUNDS   Mineral collectors will find agate and jasper in the gravel of Hixon and Ahbau Creeks (north of Quesnel), the Cottonwood River and other streams around Quesnel. Small grains of amber have been reported from lignite beds on the south bank of the Quesnel River and diatomite, formed of the skeletons of microscopic diatoms, may be found in a quarry on the big bend of the Fraser River north of the town of Quesnel. Diatomite is used in the manufacture of specialty insulating firebrick and for certain concrete applications. It is a superb insulator and in its more refined form is a good filter, due to the millions of tiny air spaces provided by the countless tiny skeletons. Diatomaceous earth is also used as a possible substitute for DDT, which has been found so harmful to our environment.

SUB-ALPINE FOREST ZONE   Once again we have changed our vegetation zone as we travel north. This is the third since Cache Creek. This zone is classed as the Engelmann Spruce alpine forest lying above the Interior Wet Belt Zone, and the two we have already seen, the Dry Interior Zone and the Cariboo Parklands Zone, and below the alpine slopes. Winters are cold, summers moderate and annual precipitation over 50 inches per year.

ENGELMANN SPRUCE   One of the dominant trees of this zone and one of the most beautiful trees in B.C. A mountain species, it grows to a height of 100 to 150 feet with a diameter of 1½ to 3½ feet. The leaves are needle-like, 4-sided, usually blunt-pointed, soft and flexible, ½ to 1 inch long and bluish green. They give off a disagreeable odor when crushed. Spruce is one of the most important trees in the

Interior of B.C., being used for general construction, finishing and pulp. It grows as a climax forest, that is, one which has evolved and left only the vegetation best suited to the climate and soil.

BLACK TWINBERRY This bush honeysuckle bears twin yellow flowers followed by black berries with reddish capes. Indians claimed that the fruit, if eaten, would cause insanity. Black twinberry, *Lonicera involucrata,* is also called Bearberry honeysuckle.

Mile 198.4
Quesnel River Crossing.

A pack-train of mules crossing the Quesnel River at Quesnel in 1868. Vancouver City Archives photo.

Mile 198.6
QUESNEL Entry in the journal of Simon Fraser, Monday August 1st, 1808.

"Set out early. Debarked at Quesnel's River where we found some of the natives, from whom we procured some furs, plenty of fish and berries. Continued our route until sunset."

The man for whom Fraser named this river, and from whom the town got its name, was Jules Maurice Quesnel, a clerk of the North West Company and Fraser's third in charge on the historic trip to the Pacific.

For many years the town was referred to as Quesnelle Mouth, distinguishing it from Quesnelle Forks, but in the early 1900's the post office changed and shortened the name.

Near the bridge crossing to the west bank of the Fraser is a Cornish water wheel such as was used by the gold miners. A working wheel is located at Barkerville. This bridge and road lead to the Blackwater and Nazko country on the Fraser and Nechako Plateaus. The area is generally wooded with many small lakes and a great many stretches of marsh and bog. It is an excellent region for moose hunting in the fall. Rich Hobson approached the Blackwater from Anahim Lake in the Chilcotin and wrote of his experiences in *"Grass Beyond the Mountains"*, *"Nothing Too Good For a Cowboy"* and *"Rancher Takes a Wife"*. .

Quesnel was also the terminus for the ill-fated Collins Overland Telegraph and a cairn near the Cornish pump pays tribute:

"After the failure of the Atlantic cable, 1858, a plan was made to connect America and Asia by telegraph and cable across the Bering Strait. In 1865-66 the wire was strung from the southern boundary of British Columbia to the Skeena River. The success of the 1866 cable ended the scheme and the line was abandoned at Quesnel. This was the first unit on the telegraph system of the West."

When the line was abandoned it was only one-quarter complete and had cost 3 million dollars. Tons of supplies were left in the bush along the route to rot and deteriorate.

Today Quesnel has a population of over 6000 people, a two-million dollar pulp mill and over 150 sawmills operating in the vicinity. As in the days of the gold rush Quesnel is the gateway to Barkerville, with many motels, hotels and tourist services to accommodate the traveller.

A museum is located near the approach to town. Continue through town for Prince George or the road to Barkerville.

Mile 202

Junction of Highway 97 and the old Cariboo road to Barkerville, Highway number 26. Our mileage follows the route of the original Cariboo Wagon Road, with the highway to Prince George being described at the end of the road as a side trip.

Ten Mile Lake Provincial Park and campground just a few miles north of Quesnel is a favourite summer swimming hole.

Mile 215

The Cottonwood River takes its name from the black cottonwood trees which grow in the area. *Populus trichocarpa* is the largest of our native poplars and is one of the fastest growing hardwoods, reaching a height of 80 to 125 feet and a diameter of 3 to 4 feet. Like most of the poplar family it requires moist soil in which to grow and is usually found in river bottom-lands. The cottonwood is very intolerant of shade and only survives by its rapid growth which enables it to keep ahead of and higher than other tree species. It is the most important broad-leafed tree in B.C. with its wood being used for boxes, veneer and plywood. Its leaves are easy to recognize. They are 3 to 5 inches long, fine-toothed; dark green, smooth above, paler, silver-white or rusty brown below. On young trees the bark is smooth and greenish yellow and on old trees, dark and deeply furrowed.

Cottonwood River Bridge on Highway 97,
a good swimming spot on a hot summer day.

Mile 215.9   Stop of Interest

Cottonwood House. For over half a century the Boyd family operated this haven for man and beast. Here weary travellers found lodging, food and drink. Here fresh horses were hitched to the stagecoach and miners bought supplies. This historic road house, built in 1864, stood as an oasis of civilization on the frontier of a rich new land.

From the time he built Cottonwood House until his death in 1909, J. Boyd kept a daily journal in which he recorded everything that happened—from guests to the amount of snow. The 34 volumes are now in the possession of the Quesnel Historical Society.

MOOSE   On this stretch of road from Quesnel to Barkerville you are likely to see the largest antlered animal in the world—an animal that has changed little since prehistoric times, *Aleces Aleces,* the moose.

The best time to see him is in the early hours of dawn or again around dusk and the best place is in the bogs, swamps and muskeg, or the trees around these spots. If it is summer the moose will quite likely be standing well above his knees in water, feeding on the aquatic plant life of the pond bottom.

Bull Moose

Moose are actually new to this part of B.C. As the ranchers and miners opened up and burned the once heavy forests, new trees started up, trees more suitable as food for the moose, like aspen and willow. In fact the Indians of the Cariboo have no word for moose in their native tongue and it wasn't until 1901 that moose were seen in Barkerville. In 1912 they reached Horsefly and Likely, Williams Lake in 1923 and Clinton in 1924. Before this time moose were mainly north of Prince George.

Mile 229.5

WINGDAM, a community and mine on Lightning Creek. October 1863. The account of Dr. Cheadle and Viscount Milton:

"The road was very rough, a narrow pack-trail out through the woods; the stumps of the felled trees were left in the ground and the thick stratum of mud in the spaces between was ploughed into deep holes by the continual trampling of mules.

. . . By the road side lay the dead bodies of horses and mules, some standing as they had died, still stuck fast in the deep tenacious mud. We passed a score of them in one day in full view; and hundreds, which had turned aside to die, lay hidden in the forest which shut in the trail so closely."

At the time that this was written, Viscount Milton was 23 years old and his tutor, Dr. Cheadle, was 27. They had come this far and reached Barkerville after incredible hardship, and near starvation on a couple of occasions.

EDIBLE PLANTS   Many of the plants and bushes you see on the side of the roads and on the hills and fields were used by the native people of B.C. for food. Tiger-lily, wild onion, wild carrot, bracken-root, wild turnip and parsnips and wild clover were harvested, dried and stored. Many berries were eaten fresh but large quantities were also dried, like our currants and raisins, or made into a dried jellied material to be used in winter. Hazelnuts and kernels of the white and yellow pine cones were also used, usually being roasted and mixed with berries.

SPRUCE TEA   Made by steeping the young twigs and leaves (needles) of spruce, hemlock, balsam fir, pine or even birch. It is an antiscorbutic (prevents scurvy) and is quite agreeable, especially when served hot with sugar.

LABRADOR TEA   This tea is made from the bush of the same name, a low-branched, aromatic shrub with evergreen, leathery, canoe-shaped leaves covered on the underside by a dense, rust covered felt. The leaves may be gathered and dried at any time of the year and then used for tea. The shrub is usually found in bogs, swamps, muskegs, moist woods and meadows.

Mile 231.4

BLESSING'S GRAVE   In 1883, a native of Ohio by the name of C. M. Blessing landed at Yale on his way to the mines. He joined up with two other men, Moses, a negro barber, and Barry, whom Blessing staked and fed all the way to Quesnel. Blessing and Barry stopped here due to sore feet while Moses went on to Barkerville. He opened a barber shop but when Blessing didn't show up after a few days as promised he began to worry. Two weeks later Barry came into town dressed in fine clothes with an abundance of American double eagle coins, saying that Blessing had returned to Yale. Moses was suspicious but had no proof until a nugget in the shape of an angel, which Blessing had prized, showed up in the possession of a hurdy-gurdy girl. She admitted Barry gave it to her and soon after police found Blessing's body, shot in the back and rolled off the road. Barry almost escaped, only being apprehended as he boarded the steamer at Yale. Tried by Judge Begbie he was hanged at the Richfield courthouse. A set of stairs in the left bank of the road led to the picketed plot of Blessing's grave.

Mile 232.6

PINEGROVE, an abandoned settlement. In 1862 this stopping place on Lightning Creek was built by 'Bloody' Edwards, an Englishman who came by his nickname because of his constant use of the word 'bloody', in such phrases as "a bloody fine day", "three bloody good cheers for the Queen", and so on.

In 1868 he sold the building to J. Hamilton, who gave it the name of "Pinegrove". There is little evidence of the buildings left.

MARTEN   Early travellers along this section of road mention seeing numerous marten, a member of the weasel family, slightly larger than a squirrel, which dwells in the pine and spruce forests of North America. Trapping has exterminated this valuable fur-bearer over much of its former range but at the best of times he was an elusive, difficult animal to view; so much so in fact that one would wonder if perhaps these travellers from other lands were mistaking our squirrels for martens. In any event it is highly doubtful if you will see one today without a lot of diligent searching.

Mile 236

BEAVER PASS   Once the site of a famous roadhouse which col- lapsed a few years ago. A side road to the north at this point leads to the headwaters of the Willow River and the Quesnel Highlands.

Cost of living got you down? Why not go back to the 'good old days' of the Cariboo gold rush. Candles were $100 for a 100-pound box. Butter was $5.00 per pound and the same for nails. Flour was $2.00 per pound and potatoes $115 per hundred pounds. Gum boots $42.50 a pair, a box of matches $1.50 and champagne 2 oz. of gold per pint!

Mile 242.5 Stop of Interest

"STANLEY CEMETERY Gold was found in nearby Lightning Creek in 1861, resulting in the towns of Stanley and Van Winkle springing up. This hilltop cemetery likely came into being soon after . . . Here lies Harry Jones, a beloved Cariboo pioneer, beside him is buried Captain John Evans, leader of 26 Welsh miners, 'The Welsh Adventurers' . . . The open pits of 36 Chinese graves indicate that the bones have been dug up long ago . . . These were shipped to Victoria, then to Hong Kong, and finally distributed for burial in the family plot. The Chinese Consolidated Benevolent Association looked after the complete details of the move."

Mile 242.7

STANLEY is now just another deserted ghost town. In the early days of the gold rush it was a boisterous camp with many bars, saloons, hotels, stores, hurdy-gurdy girls and unwashed miners. A section of Lightning Creek two miles above here yielded 8 million dollars in gold.

Stanley in 1899. Another photo by J. H. Blome. Vancouver City Archives photo.

The OLD WAGON ROAD on the hill to the left is the original route of the Cariboo road to the mines. At that time it passed through Stanley, Van Winkle, Richfield, Barkerville and Camerontown in that order. The new road via Wells was built in 1885.

Mile 250.1

JACK OF CLUBS LAKE If the government campgrounds are full, closer to Barkerville, it is usually possible to find a rough one around the lake or farther east on the side of the road. If you didn't bring insect repellant you will wish you had in this country. A collection of black flies, no-see-ums and mosquitoes can make life miserable for the unprepared cheechako. Flies are often the cause of caribou and moose running madly trying to shake off or lose the irritating, swarming hordes, usually to no avail. In fact, it isn't entirely uncommon for a city-dweller, in the bush for the first time, to do much the same thing. Your best bet is to find a breeze or take to the rivers and lakes for the fly season. For this reason late summer and fall are popular times for travel in the northeastern section of the province.

Mile 252.1

WELLS, with the Cariboo Gold Quartz mine on the right. This gold was a late comer, not being discovered until 1933 by Fred Wells. Here was found lode gold, buried deep in Cow Mountain. Cariboo Gold Quartz started work that year and in 1934 a second firm began work on Island Mountain, a 6,000-foot mountain to the north of town.

Mile 255

Take the left fork for Bowron Lakes Provincial Park, 18 miles. This 297,000-acre park was established in 1961 and the park's unique circuit of lakes makes it a favorite for canoeists. A complete round trip takes from 7 to 10 days through wilderness country with little development.

The park is named for John Bowron, a native of Huntingdon, Quebec, who was one of the original Overlanders of 1862, a party that travelled to the Cariboo gold fields by way of the Yellowhead Pass. Bowron later became postmaster of Barkerville in 1866, mining recorder in 1872, government agent in 1875 and gold commissioner in 1883, retiring in 1905.

OVERLANDERS The story of these people, unskilled in the ways of the wilderness, greenhorns, tenderfeet, is the story of a misrepresented land of fortune and an easy trail to the West. What was to have been a comfortable journey turned into one of death and privation, struggle and famine, with the coming of winter. Many of those who survived made their way home again as quickly as possible. Others, finding the gold fields not up to their expectations, turned to ranching and farming and became the founders of many of our present ranches and businesses.

Mile 255.5

CAMERONTOWN A few months after Billy Barker made his strike, John A. 'Cariboo' Cameron found gold a mile downstream. The strike brought gold but not the expected happiness, as Cameron's wife Sophia died a short time after.

In March of 1863 John disinterred her body with the intention of sending it home to Cornwall, Ontario. Upon arriving in Victoria the body waited another nine months before being shipped east. She was buried, but just about this time a rumour was started that gold and not Sophia was in the casket. Once again she was disinterred and the story proved false.

John Cameron's luck went from bad to worse and, returning to Barkerville in hopes of striking it rich again, he died penniless on November 7, 1888. His body rests in the small cemetery behind his claim and the site of Camerontown. This was the Barkerville cemetery, purchased by Cameron, who with the help of the other residents always kept the graves in a neat and tidy fashion. A sign is erected here which reads:

'One of 'Cariboo' Cameron's men died and they hauled him up the side hill and planted him there' . . . Fred Tregillus. And so this historic cemetery came into being with the burial of Peter Gibson, 31 years of age on July 24th, 1863. The great and the not so great from the gold rush era lie in this peaceful setting . . . Please respect these consecrated acres with their time-honored tributes to those that forever have a place in Barkerville.

Mile 255

BARKERVILLE The end of the road and the end of our journey. A cairn here is inscribed as follows:

"Cariboo Gold Fields. The center of old Cariboo, whose gold fields, discovered in 1861, have added over forty millions to the wealth of the world. Here was the terminus of the Great Wagon Road from Yale, completed in 1865. The story of the Cariboo Gold Mines and the Cariboo Road is the epic of British Columbia."

Anyone visiting this fascinating area would be well advised to pick up a copy of Bruce Ramsey's *A Guide to Barkerville* published by Mitchell Press. Complete with many photos of the early days it will make any visit much more enjoyable and educational.

Barkerville, the end of the trail, Eldorado for thousands of hopeful miners.
Vancouver City Archives photo.

Horse races in Barkerville in 1898 drew everyone's attention. Races were held on the main street and usually on either the Queen's birthday or Dominion Day.
Vancouver City Archives photo.

DUTCH BILL In February of 1861 William 'Dutch Bill' Dietz and his party left the town of Antler Creek and hiked over the hump in search of another strike. After panning several creeks and streams Bill found one yielding about $1.50 to the pan. The miners named the creek Williams Creek and Dutch Bill returned to Antler for more supplies, trying not to spread any word of his strike in the town. But miners are not a trusting lot and many of them had the feeling that Dutch Bill was on to something, so they tracked him through the

A miner on the Caledonia claim using a hand rocker for washing gold. 1868. Vancouver City Archives photo.

snow back to his findings and another rush for the creeks was on. The new town was called Williams Creek and later Richfield; it was located one mile north of Barkerville.

BILLY BARKER   Sometime during the next couple of years Billy Barker arrived at Williams Creek and started a new type of operation. They all laughed as Billy started to dig, but when he hit paydirt, resting on the bedrock at 52 feet, no one was merry except him. Leaving a town named after him which had grown around his claim, he went to Victoria where he married a widow by the name of Elizabeth Collyer. She and the bars took all the money he had and left him broke. He returned, as so many did, to try again for a few years, but his later efforts were unsuccessful and he died a pauper in Victoria in 1894.

BARKERVILLE   On September 16, 1868, Barkerville burned to the ground, destroying 116 buildings at a value of $700,000. The fire was supposed to have been started when a miner, trying to kiss a hurdy-gurdy girl, knocked over a stove and chimney.

By the next morning the town was starting to rebuild and this time the houses and streets were much better laid out. The main street was 15 feet wider, sidewalks were more uniform and side streets were allowed for. A week after the fire there were already 30 buildings erected.

After the gold petered out the town of Barkerville was gradually deserted, leaving only a few miners searching for the mother lode or making a meager living repanning the gravel. Fred Tregillus was one of those who stayed. He later found his part of the lode and sold it for enough money to keep him the rest of his days.

When the mines opened up around Jack of Clubs Lake and in Wells, many of the new hardrock miners came to occupy with squatter's rights the old homes of Barkerville and once again the town was inhabited.

In 1962 Barkerville was officially opened as an historic provincial park. The town has been restored to a period after the great fire and before 1880. Here with costumed actors, impersonating Judge Begbie and the stage driver, you can relive the days of the gold strike. You may walk the dusty streets, the boardwalks and along the creek on the piles of gravel from the placer mining. In fact, you can even try your hand at panning and eat bacon and beans in the Wake-up Jake Saloon.

In any town with the history that Barkerville has you will hear tall tales, anecdotes and interesting bits of gossip that have filtered down from the early days. Many such stories can be found in the book 'Barkerville Days' by Fred Ludditt.

One old custom of the town was that one never put less than $2.00 in the church collection plate. No one seems to know how the custom got started but it was carried on during the second gold rush in the depression years.

SNOWFALL   The average snowfall in Barkerville is 188 inches. The maximum recorded is 258 inches. The roads are kept open all year.

 DEATH AND DISEASE   A walk through any one of the cemeteries in Barkerville, Stanley or by a small lonely grave beside a trail will give evidence of what a harsh life it was in the early years. Many of the markers record ages of under thirty, often twenty or less. Medical care was almost non-existent. Mining accidents, cold winters and scurvy took a heavy toll of life.

 CARIBOO   The story of the name 'Cariboo' is not simply that illiterate miners couldn't spell properly but rather a story illustrating the good humor and practical jokes of men in a rough land always ready for a laugh.

It seems that there was a magistrate living on Williams Creek in the early days by the name of Cox. He was known as a bit of a boaster, a braggart. One day he bragged that he could shoot a caribou on the edge of town. Challenged, he laid a bet on it and the practical jokers of town got to work.

The story goes that several of the men went into the hills and shot a bull, brought him back to the road just out of town and propping him up, tied a length of rope around his neck. Up the road came the judge, looking for an easy kill and there it was, a lovely bull. He fired, the rope was pulled, and down came the caribou. The miners carried the animal back to town for Cox, as he hurried to spread word of his prowess as a hunter.

The story was told that evening in the bar, and repeated up and down the trails for weeks. Cox, growing weary of the laughter at his expense, would shout, before anyone could ask him about his hunting trip,

"Cariboo, Cariboo, Cari boo, boo, boooo!"

The joke wore out, but the name Cariboo stuck.

 GOLD DEPOSITS   Millions of years ago deposits of gold were formed in the Cariboo, when dinosaurs still roamed this primeval land. During this time the gold was freed from its original veins and washed into the river beds. As the river beds were covered with

alluvial deposits of gravel the gold became buried deep in the earth. When our present land mass was formed some of these old river beds were pushed toward the surface.

Then the glaciers advanced across the continent out of the North. They cut the mountains, spread more deposits on the creeks and as new streams and rivers formed they picked up the particles of gold, depositing them in the sand bars from Williams Creek to the sea. But these findings, these deposits, were only the surface gold. Most of it lay deep down on the old bedrock where men like Billy Barker found it after hard digging.

The original gold lay buried in the ore veins of the hard rock and it is these twisted, broken faults and veins that are being mined today. This is the mother lode that the miners searched for so long and so hard.

Gold strikes similar to those at Wells had already been found in the Bridge River region around Lillooet. They formed the basis of the Pioneer and Bralorne mines.

And so we have reached the end of the Cariboo road, 260 miles from Cache Creek in the Dry Interior belt to the Subalpine forest of Barkerville.

The description that follows is for the modern traveller who may be coming to Barkerville as a side trip and not looking at it as the end of his journey. The mileage picks up at Quesnel and continues on to Prince George.

Mile 208.3

TEN MILE LAKE PARK A popular swimming hole for the residents of Quesnel and at last report was still under construction. There are 39 campsites and 21 picnic tables available but you should carry your own drinking water.

Mile 212.2

COTTONWOOD RIVER and bridge, just downstream from the P.G.E.'s high level bridge.

Stop of Interest

BRIDGING THE COTTONWOOD Plans to complete the Pacific Great Eastern railroad to Prince George in 1921 failed because unstable ground prevented use of the proposed bridge site on the Cottonwood River. Thus construction stopped at Quesnel. As northern expansion continued, the need for this rail link increased and a successful upstream crossing was completed in 1952.

Drinking water is available on the right at the far side of the bridge.

OWLS There is a story about owls that when the world was created all the birds had feathers except the owl, because there were just not enough to go around. The rest of the birds agreed to give the owl a few feathers each and he in return promised to repay them as soon as he could. But the owl never did. And that is why to this day all the birds are continually fighting and chasing the owl.

Crows and jays in particular frequently chase and harass owls, particularly the great horned owl. This large, savage, powerful bird preys on a variety of small animals and birds — one of which is the crow. Should a crow spot a dozing owl he lets out a particularly intonated caw that calls all other crows in the area. They gather as close to the dozing owl as possible and caw as loudly as only crows can. When the poor owl has had enough of this cacophony he leaves, escorted by a flock of black pursuers.

It is this owl, the great horned owl, that you are most likely to see in the Cariboo. He is 18 to 25 inches tall, grey in color with distinctive 'horns' on top of his head. The owls range over all of Canada and usually nest while snow is still on the ground, in either an old crow or hawk nest. Sometimes they will use a cavity in a tree, laying two or three white eggs which hatch in 30 days. Owls are protected along with all other birds of prey, including the raven.

Mile 223.4

This side road leads 6 miles west to the community of CINEMA, which was named by Dr. Lloyd Champlain who thought this would be a good place to make motion pictures. Near Cinema is a B.C. government campsite, Cottonwood River Park. It has 9 sites, drinking water and fishing.

Mile 227.5

THE B.C. FOREST SERVICE NAVER-AHBAU ACCESS ROAD. This wilderness region is a favorite with hunters in the fall and can be enjoyed particularly by those with a boat. Twenty-one miles down the road, after passing Ahbau, Hay and Lodi Lakes, we come to the Willow River. From here you can go downstream a few miles to where Stephanie Creek joins the Willow, then up the creek to Stony Lake. At the end of this five-mile lake a creek leads to Rond Lake and Stephen Lake. Moose are quite common in this area and the lakes are good on the troll for char fishing.

Ahbau Lake is named after a Chinese prospector and trapper who lived here and reportedly had a liking for poker and strong drink.

Mile 228

STRATHNAVER, a small community and railway station, is named for the Scottish estate of the Duke of Sutherland who visited Canada In 1909 and purchased 4000 acres in this area. His plan was to colonize the valley with Scottish settlers. The name means 'a valley with a river running through it'.

BEAR   Although they are not frequently seen, black bears are common throughout most of B.C. They are not always black but may be brown or cinnamon, or even white like the Kermodi on the coast. Grizzly are no longer as plentiful as they once were due to their need to be alone with nature. There are few places where modern man allows this.

Cinnamon color phase of the Black Bear.

Early settlers in the Cariboo used the bear for many purposes. They ate the meat, used the fat as a cure-all for cuts and burns, as axle grease and for candles, soap and hair oil. The skins were welcome in cold weather and were made up into coats and bed-covers.

In fact even the excrement had a use. William Byrd, an early historian, wrote: "Bears are black and so is their dung but it will make linen white, being a tolerable soap without any preparation except drying."

Mile 238.4
HIXON   A small highway community

Mile 240.7
HIXON CREEK   Named after Joseph Foster Hixon, who led a party of miners to the area on June 27, 1866.

Mile 244.5

WOODPECKER   A station of the P.G.E., takes its name from Woodpecker Island which lies slightly to the south in the Fraser River. The island is said to have got its name from the sound of Chinese labourers cutting cordwood for the steamships, which used the island for a fuel stop.

Mile 256.7

STONE CREEK OR BUCKHORN FORESTRY ACCESS ROAD, heading through the Naver Pulp Harvesting Forest, across the lower slopes of Mount George, to a number of fishing lakes. Grizzly, Ste. Marie, Narrow, Fish, Pitoney, Wansa and Hidden are all good lakes for trolling with some spin or fly casting.

Mile 257.4
STONER   This community is another small supply point for mills and farms.

History is somewhat lacking in this part of the country for it has only recently been opened up. Before the day of the P.G.E. and the roads the only travel was by river; such were the routes of the Frasers, the Thompsons and Mackenzies.

Mile 272.2

Junction. The secondary route to Prince George is the old road. It passes the airport and the Federal experimental farm and provides access to the newly completed road to McBride, Jasper and Kamloops, Highway 16. It saves 400 miles for those wishing to travel to Edmonton.

Mile 277.6

The junction of the Fraser and Nechako Rivers.

PRINCE GEORGE   The first white man to pass by this junction was Alexander Mackenzie in 1793, when, 12 years before Lewis and Clark, he crossed the North American Continent by land. Then in 1807 Simon Fraser built a fort here as a trading post and a base for his exploration of the Fraser River and a route to the sea. When he embarked on his history-making voyage from here in 1808 he left Hugh Farris in charge. At that time the post was without a name.

Later in 1828 Sir George Simpson mentioned Fort George in his letters to London concerning what he had found during his voyage down the Fraser. He wrote:

"We have it likewise in view, to re-establish the Post of Fort George, which was abandoned in the year 1823 in consequence of the Murder of two of our people by the Natives; which may be expected to yield about 25 Packs Furs; 12 to 15 of which, now go to other Posts, so that the re-establishment of this place will probably encrease (sic) the returns by about 12 packs, value about 1000 (pounds)."

For many years Prince George, now no longer a Fort, grew slowly, almost imperceptibly. Then in the 1960's the rush for the North was on. Many mills opened up and with the establishment of three pulp mills employment swelled and housing became harder and harder to find. But the town caught up to the rush and is now one of the largest in B.C. — and still growing.

Bibliography

AKRIGG, G. P. V. and Helen B. *1001 B.C. Place Names.* Discovery Press Van 1969.

BANDONI, Robert J. and SZCZAWINSKI, Adam F. *Guide to Common Mushrooms of British Columbia.* B.C. Provincial Museum 1964.

BEESON, Edith. *Dunlevy, from the Diaries of Alex P. McInnes.* Lillooet Publishers, 1971.

BOUVETTE, W. S. *The True Story of the Cariboo Wagon Road.* Pamphlet.

B.C. Provincial Museum, *Our Native Peoples — B.C. Heritage Series:*
Vol. 2 *Coast Salish.*
Vol. 3 *Interior Salish 1952.*
Vol. 9 *Déné 1953.*

CARAS, Roger A. *North American Mammals.* Meredith Press 1967.

CARL, G. Clifford. *The Reptiles of British Columbia.* B.C. Provincial Museum 1960.
—With CLEMENS, W. A. and LINDSEY, C.C. *The Fresh-water Fishes of British Columbia.* B.C. Provincial Museum.

CLINE, Sperry. *Cataline.* B.C. Outdoors. Dec. 1970.

CORNER, John. *Pictographs in the Interior of B.C.* 1968.

COWAN, Ian McTaggart and GUIGUET, Charles J. *The Mammals of B.C.* B.C. Provincial Museum 1965.

DEPARTMENT OF PUBLIC WORKS — Magazine. *Mileposts on the Cariboo Road.* July 1939.

DEMARCHI, Dennis A. Personal correspondence Dec. 11, 1970.

DOWNS, Art. *Wagon Road North.* Northwest Digest Ltd., Surrey, B.C. 1963.

FORBES, F. G. (Molly). Personal correspondence Dec. 1970 *Lac La Hache. Historical notes on the early settlers.* Pamphlet.

FRASER, Simon. *Letters and Journals 1806-1808.* Edited by W. Kaye Lamb. MacMillan 1960

Geographic Board of Canada Reports. Queen's Printer.

GODFREY, W. Earl. *The Birds of Canada.* Queen's Printer—Ottawa 1966.

GRUNDLE, Jack. Editor. *Western Fish and Game 1971 B.C. Fishing Guide.*

GUIGET, Charles J. *The Birds of British Columbia.* B.C. Provincial Museum 1960.

HUBBARD, William A. *The Grasses of British Columbia.* B.C. Provincial Museum 1969.

HUTCHINSON, Bruce. *The Fraser.* Clarke Irwin, Toronto-Vancouver 1950-1965.

LINDSAY, F. W. *The Cariboo Story.*
Cariboo Yarns.
The Outlaws. Lytton, B.C.

LYONS, Chess. *Milestones on the Mighty Fraser.* 1950.
Trees, Flowers and Shrubs to Know in B.C. Dent 1952.

McDONALD, Archibald. *Peace River — A Canoe Voyage from Hudson's Bay to the Pacific in 1828.* Coles 1970.

MILLS, Alan and RAY, Raoul. *Canadian Folk Songs: A Centennial Collection.* C.B.C. and R.C.A. Victor.

MILTON, Viscount, and CHEADLE, W. B., MA. M.D. *The North-West Passage By Land.* London 1865. Coles 1970.

ORMSBY, Margaret A. *British Columbia: A History.* MacMillan — 1964.

RAMSEY, Bruce. *Ghost Towns of B.C.* 1963 Mitchell Press.
History on the Highways. Province 1958.
A Guide to Barkerville. Mitchell Press.
Mining in Focus 1968.

ROBERTS, Anna. *Birds of the Cariboo.* April 1970. Dept. Continuing Education. Williams Lake, B.C.

SABINA, Anna P. *Rock and Mineral Collecting in Canada.* Geological Survey of Canada, Vol. 1. Queen's Printer 1965.

SISMEY, Eric D. *Chinook Jargon.* Canada West Magazine, Summer 1969.

SMITH, Keith C. Personal Communications. January 1970.

SZCZAWINSKI, Adam F. and HARDY, George A. *Guide to Common Edible Plants of B.C.* B.C. Provincial Museum 1962.

TEIT, J. A. *Publications of the Jessup North Pacific Expedition.* American Museum of Natural History, 1900.

WRIGHT, Richard and Rochelle. *Pelicans of Stum.* B.C. Outdoors, April 1970.
Chilcotin Country. Canadian Outdoorsman, December 1968.
Death of the Rivers. Western Fish & Game, September 1969.
Cariboo Highway: Mileposts to History. B.C. Outdoors, Part 1, April 1972. Part 2, June 1972.

PERIODICALS consulted:

B.C. Motorist	*Ashcroft Journal*
B.C. Outdoors	*Williams Lake Tribune*
Western Fish & Wildlife	*100 Mile House Free Press*
Canada West Magazine	*Clinton-Cache Creek Pioneer*
Wildlife Review	

Index